favorite FABRIC

BOWLS, BOXES & VASES

15 QUICK-TO-MAKE PROJECTS • 45 INSPIRING VARIATIONS

LINDA JOHANSEN

C&T PUBLISHING

Text copyright © 2016 by Linda Johansen

Photography and artwork copyright © 2016 by C&T Publishing, Inc.

Publisher: Amy Marson

Creative Director: Gailen Runge

Editors: Joanna Burgarino, Liz Aneloski, Cyndy Lyle Rymer, and Eleanor Levie from Craft Services, LLC

Technical Editors: Carolyn Aune, Robin Gronning, Gailen Runge, Joyce Engels Lytle, and Eleanor Levie from Craft Services, LLC

Cover Designer: April Mostek

Book Designer: Kristen Yenche

Production Coordinators: Zinnia Heinzmann and Freesia Pearson Blizard

Production Editors: Joanna Burgarino, Alice Mace Nakanishi, and Jennifer Warren

Illustrators: Kerry Graham, Shawn Garcia, Tim Manibusan, and Kirstie L. Pettersen

Photo Assistant: Sarah Frost

Photography by Diane Pedersen, unless otherwise noted

Published by C&T Publishing, Inc., P.O. Box 1456, Lafayette, CA 94549

Library of Congress Cataloging-in-Publication Data

Names: Johansen, Linda, 1951- author.

Title: Favorite fabric bowls, boxes & vases : 15 quick-to-make projects - 45 inspiring variations / Linda Johansen.

Other titles: Favorite fabric bowls, boxes and vases

Description: Lafayette, CA : C&T Publishing, Inc., [2016] | Includes bibliographical references and index.

Identifiers: LCCN 2016003427 | ISBN 9781617452499 (soft cover : alk. paper)

Subjects: LCSH: Textile crafts. | Machine sewing. | Bowls (Tableware) | Boxes. | Vases.

Classification: LCC TT699 .J626 2016 | DDC 746.4--dc23

LC record available at http://lccn.loc.gov/2016003427

Printed in China

10 9 8 7 6 5 4 3 2 1

ACKNOWLEDGMENTS

I owe a great many thanks to the following people:

- My life partner—Jay Thatcher—on our new journey together without kids

- My kids—Jay Johansen; his wife, Terra Leven; and Evan Thatcher—without you I wouldn't be who I am

- An honorary kid and friend—Merka Martin—who knows just when to call and lift me up

- The Border Collie girls—Echo, 9; Djinn, 10; and Pita, 13¾—the stitches that keep a smile on my face and my floor clean

- The gals—Alex Vincent, Sidnee Snell, Kim Campbell, and Libby Ankarberg—the angels who kept me sane through five of the books

- Cindy Crook—you know why

- The store owners and staff who believed in me before I did—Jessica Yorgey and Geary Cuniff of Quiltwork Patches in Corvallis, Barb Schriener of BJ's Quilt Basket in Bend, and Laura Wallace Dickson and Jan Raith at A Common Thread in Lake Oswego

- The great folks at C&T—too many to list, and they're all wonderful

- All of you who have enjoyed my books and sent me photos and wonderful notes—knowing that my books have brought you joy means more than you can imagine

Thank you, all!

contents

introduction

I was either born with, or trained to have, an insatiable curiosity. I started making fabric bowls after seeing a student's bowl during a class. I have had so much fun with the instant gratification of making fabric bowls, as well as the artistic side of combining fabrics and threads and shaping a bowl to fit my mood at the time. I use the bowls throughout my house as functional art on tables and counters—holding treasures, candles, and food. As I played with making fabric bowls and taught others how to make them, more possibilities kept popping into my head. It was a natural progression to leap from fabric bowls to fabric boxes. Just seeing leftover food in a paper takeout box was enough to inspire me to design the To-Go Box (page 56)! Plus, the boxes are so easy that you can make one in a day and still have time to "really" quilt!

I strongly believe that part of our purpose here on earth is to create beauty. When I can combine beauty with function, the results are deeply satisfying for me. My goal with my first books, the Fast, Fun & Easy series in the 2000s, was to help others bring the beauty of fabric into their decor. I am thrilled to revitalize that goal by using new fabrics to share the beauty of my favorite fabric container designs with a brand-new audience.

Through all my books, I have had the joy of working with a small group of dedicated fiber artists. You will see some of their work throughout the book. These women took my written instructions and then experimented with a bunch of new ideas. If you're trying out these bowls, boxes, and vases for the first time, or even if you're a pro, I really encourage you to gather a group of friends around you who enjoy fabric arts. You can challenge each other, and the brainstorming that can happen will elevate your work far beyond what you could imagine. The ideas for variations just kept coming, which is why we felt now was a good time to reintroduce our favorite bowls so that you can adapt them to your own style!

I don't expect you to always follow the directions. They are here as guidelines—to help you make that first box (or two, or three) and see how it all works. You can mix and match the techniques in the book however you like.

Read through All the Basics (page 5) to get an overview of the materials and techniques. Then, try your hand at some of the simpler bowls, boxes, and vases that start off each section. After you feel comfortable and confident, mix and match the instructions and embellish to your heart's content.

I hope you will enjoy making these bowls, boxes, and vases as much as I have over the years. And when you're finished, I'd love to see pictures! Please post photos of your finished projects on Instagram using #FabricBowlsBoxesVases.

I can't wait to see your variations!

Never stop creating!

Linda

all the basics

Here's a handy guide on choosing materials and supplies and learning basic techniques. Give it a quick read; then refer back here whenever you need some extra help.

MATERIALS AND SUPPLIES

All the projects call for "basic supplies." This shorthand phrase refers to items you probably already own for marking, cutting, pressing, and stitching. For cutting, you'll need rotary cutting tools and scissors; for pressing, you'll need an iron, ironing surface, and products to protect both of these from the fusible web. For stitching, you'll need a sewing machine with presser feet and sewing machine needles— and a seam ripper, just in case!

FABRIC

Choose a good-quality 100% cotton fabric that you just love. Your project will last longer, and it will be easier to sew. Once you are familiar with the techniques, be brave and play with other fabric choices. If you are using a directional fabric or fussy cutting to highlight a motif, you may need to cut larger pieces.

Some fabric and thread combinations

INTERFACING

Fabric containers need something sturdy inside the layers to be able to hold their shape. Experiment with different interfacing options to find the look and feel you want for your projects. You want the material to be light, to hold its shape, to be able to take the heat of an iron, and to be washable. All the projects in this book are designed to be made with fast2fuse, Timtex, or canvas (see Resources, page 79). If a project calls for one of these three types of interfacing, you can easily switch it out for one of the other two. If you are substituting a completely different type of interfacing, make sure that it is 22″ wide so that it matches the instructions.

All these stabilizers can be quilted if you want to embellish your bowl, box, or vase.

fast2fuse

fast2fuse Double-Sided Fusible Stiff Interfacing (by C&T Publishing; available in Light, Medium, and Heavy) is a stiff interfacing with the fusible already on both sides. This interfacing really simplifies the preparation and can be used in any project in this book, even projects that call for canvas or Timtex.

If you are using fast2fuse in a project that calls for canvas or Timtex, do not purchase any fusible web, and omit the steps for fusing the web onto fabric and interfacing. Instead, fuse the fabric to both sides of the fast2fuse, using its precoated fusible. It works best if your fabric has been prewashed.

The fast2fuse Heavy works best on shapes with straight sides, while the medium weight works best on shapes with curved sides. At half the weight of fast2fuse Heavy, fast2fuse Light is probably not stiff enough for most of the projects in this book; however, it is an option if you want to experiment with creating lighter finished projects (such as for some of the bowls).

Canvas

I like to use a 10-ounce cotton duck for my canvas interfacing. Two layers of it give me a sturdier surface to work with and plenty of stiffness to hold the shape. Denim and other canvas will work as well. Do not prewash. If the fabric has been washed, you might want to apply a bit of starch to the side you are not fusing onto. Also, be sure your chosen canvas is 100% cotton—otherwise the fusible may not stick to it, and the fibers may melt under the iron. When using canvas as an interfacing, it's best to add dense lines of machine stitching to make the sides of the project firmer.

It can be helpful to secure the canvas to your fabric pieces with a temporary fabric adhesive or basting spray.

Timtex

Timtex (by C&T Publishing) is ⅛"-thick interfacing made of rayon and polyester, and it is about the same stiffness as fast2fuse Heavy. The main difference is that Timtex does not come coated with fusible. You must use a fusible web to adhere the fabric to the Timtex for the projects. Simply iron fusible web to your fabric before fusing it to the Timtex, and then follow the project directions.

Timtex holds its shape very well. Projects made with it can be washed and shaped with steam pressing. Because this stabilizer is so thick, you won't need any extra stitching to add firmness to your project.

THREADS

I recommend using either cotton or polyester thread. Choose a good-quality cotton or polyester thread, as some threads break easily with so much heavy stitching. I use Isacord or Mettler Polysheen for their strength and sheen. For satin stitch, decorative stitches, or free-motion stitching, loosen your machine's top tension to about 2.5 and use a top-stitch needle. Once you have made a couple of projects, play with some variegated and decorative threads.

> **tip THREAD TROUBLE?**
> If you are having trouble with your threads, follow these steps:
>
> 1. Rethread the top thread, and then the bobbin thread.
>
> 2. Be sure the bobbin is in all the way. If your bobbin case has a finger with a hole in the end, try threading through the hole.
>
> 3. Change the needle—be sure it's a topstitch needle.
>
> 4. Lower the tension on the top thread.
>
> If the thread still isn't doing what you want, change the thread. Don't spend your time fighting it. Use the same thread in the top and bobbin. That way, you won't have to be quite as precise with your tension.

FUSIBLE WEB

If using Timtex or canvas, you will need to use a fusible web to fuse it to the fabric. You can use any fusible that holds the layers together permanently and easily; however, a heavyweight fusible may be difficult to sew and may gum up the needle. I recommend and use Pellon Wonder-Under.

> **tip MADE A MISTAKE?**
> Cover it up! Use fusible web and a scrap of fabric to cover up any mistakes. Instead of a mistake, you'll have a beautiful embellishment! No one will ever know....

CORDING

For a nice finished look, I use cording or string around the edges of the bowls. It allows the thread to cover the edge more easily, and I find it takes less time and thread. Use a 1/16″ polyester cording (made for clothing and pillow piping), a lightweight cotton knitting yarn, a heavyweight crochet thread such as Speed-Cro-Sheen (by Coats & Clark), household string, or whatever you find that works for you. You want the cording to be about the same thickness as your bowl sandwich when you are ready to finish the edge. Avoid cording with fuzzy fibers—that's what you're trying to cover! (See Using Cording, page 9, for instructions on how to apply it.)

Craft and fabric stores carry some beautiful decorative cording and yarns that can negate the need for satin stitching. The best I've found is 1/8″ rattail cording (see Resources, page 79).

Cording will make those edges nice and smooth and strong.

SEWING MACHINE

A good, basic sewing machine that can make a straight stitch and a zigzag stitch and that uses a darning foot is all you need to make any projects in the book. Before you start any project, make sure your machine can stitch through two layers of your chosen interfacing (pages 5 and 6) and four layers of your fabric.

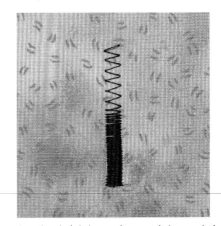

A satin stitch is just a shortened zigzag stitch.

Sewing Machine Needles

You will want a sharp needle for sewing through the layers of fabrics, fusible web, and stiff interfacing. Topstitch 80/12 or 90/14 needles work best for me and make the project go much easier. They have a wider hole and deeper slot up the back to protect the thread as it goes through the fabrics. Choose the larger size for heavier layers.

Sewing Machine Feet

You will want an open-toe embroidery foot and a darning foot. I use an open-toe foot for all the surface stitching and the satin stitching. It has space on the underside of the foot to allow for bulky stitching, and I can always see what the needle and thread are doing. The darning foot is used for decorative or free-motion stitching as directed in the projects.

SCISSORS

I keep three pairs of scissors handy: a small pair for clipping inside corners and snipping threads, cutting shears for the project pieces, and double-curved, duck-billed embroidery scissors for the final cleanup along the edges of the pieces. Whichever scissors you use, make sure they are sharp.

IRONING BOARD PROTECTIVE SHEETS

Use a protective sheet to keep your ironing board free of stray fusible web that might adhere to the outside of your projects. Keep the protective sheet under the fabric and fusible. I like to use June Tailor or Clotilde pressing sheets, or C&T Publishing's Silicone Release Paper. I also use a piece of white muslin to cover my ironing board.

ADDITIONAL SUPPLIES FOR VASES

Weights

Most of the vases will be much more stable with some sort of weight in the bottom. There are many things you can use for this—popcorn kernels, fishing weights, pie weights, nuts and bolts, small stones, floral marbles, curtain weights, or floral frogs are just a few.

Balloons

You can use balloons to round out the vases while you steam iron them to shape. Have several sizes of sturdy round balloons on hand. (You can reuse these balloons.)

BASIC TECHNIQUES

CUTTING

You can do much of the cutting with a rotary cutter, slicing through all the layers at once. However, cutting darts, snipping threads, trimming the edges of a base that's stitched down, or neatening up the edges of a bowl—all these call for cutting with scissors.

PRESSING AND FUSING

Iron your fabrics smooth before you use them in a bowl, and follow the manufacturer's instructions for the fusible web you are using. When applying fusible web, avoid getting the adhesive on your iron or ironing surface by using a pressing cloth or Teflon sheet (see Resources, page 79).

> **tip** If using Timtex or canvas, always iron the fusible web to the fabric first, and then fuse the fabric onto the Timtex or canvas. Because the fabric is thinner than Timtex or canvas, more of the iron's heat will penetrate it, which means it will fuse better.

STITCHING

The purpose of the stitching (all by machine!) is to join edges, add stability to the sides of the bowl, and provide a design element. You will want the most balanced stitches you can achieve—stitches that look neat and even from both sides of your reversible bowl.

Check your stitching for correct thread tension every time you change from straight stitch to zigzag stitch or other decorative stitches. For a bowl with overlapped darts, make sure your machine can sew neatly through a double thickness of the textile sandwich.

Lockstitches

To start and end off any satin stitches that won't be caught in subsequent lines of stitches, set your machine for the tiniest straight stitch—close to zero (0). Take a few stitches right alongside previous stitches. Clip the thread ends close to the surface.

Decorative Stitching

Contrasting thread can really add excitement to a bowl. Machine stitch a pattern of stars, a grid, or continuous concentric shapes on the base. If you enjoy free-motion quilting, or your machine does some fancy stitches, consider using a more interesting pattern. While decorative stitching can be added to the bowl at any time, it is easier to do—especially on the base—while the bowl is still flat. I add decorative stitching to the rim *after* I sew the darts.

USING CORDING

Use a cording that is slightly thinner than or the same thickness as the sandwich of fabric and interfacing layers. I like cotton cording, because it takes a colored pen better when the stitching doesn't quite cover it and I have to fill in with a pen!

Sew the cording with a zigzag stitch; then do the satin stitching as a separate step. You will not save time by trying to do it all at once. (I know from experience!)

1. Set the zigzag stitch for a 1.5 length, and keep it wide enough to catch the edge of your project and cover the cording (approximately 4.0 width).

2. Lay the cording right next to the raw edge. Hold the end of the cording behind the presser foot, and do a few zigzag stitches to hold the cording in place. Then, zigzag stitch the cording around the whole piece. Twist the cording as you sew to keep it tight.

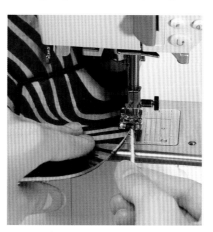

Stitching cording around the edges uses less time and thread.

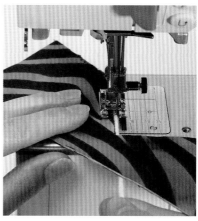

Move the cording under the bowl on inside corners or curves.

tip **If the piece you are sewing has inside corners, as you sew up to the corner pull the cording under the sandwich so that you can stitch clear to the corner (or curve). Stop with the needle down, just outside the cording at the corner. Pull the cording out from under the sandwich, and turn the sandwich so that the cording is again along the edge. Continue zigzag stitching.**

3. Clip the cording very close to the beginning stitching.

4. Sew right up to the start of the cording, and finish with more stitching in place to hold the end.

Trim the beginning and end of the cording so that no lump forms when satin stitching.

5. Once the cording is attached, satin stitch over the cording all the way around the project. Be sure your stitch is wide enough to catch the edge and cover the cording completely (approximately 4.0–4.5 width).

6. Set your sewing machine to a very fine (0.5 stitch length) straight stitch, and take a few stitches along the inside edge of the satin stitching to anchor the stitches. Then trim the thread ends closely.

MAKING CIRCLES

To make big circles, use one of the following methods:

Method 1: Use compass points and a 1″ × 12½″ rotary ruler. Set the pencil point for half the diameter of the circle you want (a 6″ setting makes a 12″ circle).

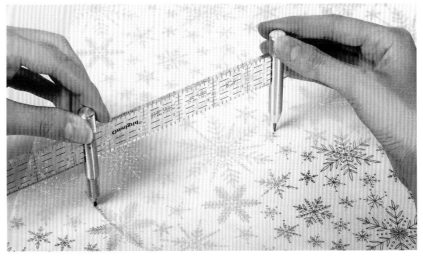

Use compass points to draw your circle; then cut it with scissors or a rotary cutter.

Method 2: Use a plate and a compass to extend the circle. Set the compass for half the extra distance you want for the whole circle (a 10″ plate would need an additional 1″ on the compass to make a 12″ circle).

Extend the circle width using a compass.

Method 3: Use a larger round template from around your home and trace around it.

To make small circles, do the following:

Use a circle cutter or circle template, or set a school compass for half the diameter you need and draw the circle.

Troubleshooting Tips

PROBLEM:
I don't like the way the base of my bowl looks.

Solution: At any point (even if the rest of the bowl is finished) you can cut a new base, back the fabric with fusible web, and iron it over the existing base. Choose a different fabric, or cover stitching that didn't work. Finish the edges with satin stitching.

PROBLEM:
I made a mistake cutting the dart.

Solutions: Try one of these suggestions.
A. Rip it out and redo it, making more or less of an overlap.
B. Trim the overlapped dart before you sew the second side.
C. If you've removed a dart, consider sewing a narrower dart back into the bowl.
D. Make more darts with the same "mistake"!

PROBLEM:
The threads show through on the other side of the bowl.

Solution: If you are having trouble with the thread on the top of your piece, check your bobbin tension and threading. If the trouble is extra thread on the underside, check your top tension and threading. For satin stitching, check to see if the arm on your bobbin case has a little hole. If it does, pass the bobbin thread through it.

PROBLEM:
My satin stitch produces big bumps of thread when I pivot to change direction.

Solution: At the corners, lift the presser foot slightly to help the bowl through, or put a scrap of the bowl sandwich under the back of the presser foot. As you overlap stitches, increase the stitch width slightly.

PROBLEM:
My needles keep breaking.

Solution: Try a larger-size needle. Let your machine do the work. Don't try to "muscle" the project. Gentle pulling may help sometimes, but if you pull when the needle is down, it will break.

FREE-MOTION QUILTING

Proper machine setup and a lot of practice are the secrets to success.

1. Lower the feed dogs on your machine. If your sewing machine doesn't have feed dogs that lower, then cover them with an index card, taped over the feed dog slots.

2. Attach a darning foot to your machine. This foot clamps the textile sandwich in place when the needle is down but releases the textile sandwich when the needle is up. You have the freedom to move the fabric in any direction while the needle is up.

3. Decrease or loosen the presser foot and upper thread tension.

4. Practice on a test sandwich similar to your fabric bowl—or on the textile sandwich that will become your fabric bowl. Move the sandwich in all directions, making straight lines, curves, or meander stitches. Adjust the tension by tiny amounts until you achieve a balanced stitch that is even on both sides. Use consistent speed, for the machine and in moving the fabric, to produce stitches that are the same length throughout.

 tip **If you forget to make lockstitches, apply a dot of liquid sealant, such as Fray Block (by June Tailor, Inc.).**

SHAPING

STEAMING

The vases will steam to shape quite nicely. Just blow up a sturdy balloon inside the vase, and hold the balloon closed while you iron with steam. For the sides, leave the balloon in while the fabric cools. Steam the base after you have done the sides, and hold it on a cool counter or other surface so that it will cool flat.

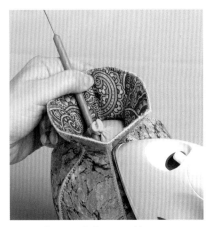

Steam the rounded vases with a balloon inside.

CREATING DARTS

Just as darts shape clothing to the contours of your body, the darts in a bowl determine its contours. If you overlap the cut edges, the bowl will be stiffer and stronger. If you cut out the dart and butt the edges together, the bowl sides will be softer and more flexible.

Most projects in this book call for a specific dart shape. However, you are the creator of your bowl. Feel free to play. To empower your creativity, refer to these bowl diagrams, which suggest the general shape of bowl you can achieve from a specific type of dart.

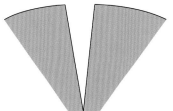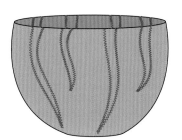

Straight darts produce a deeper bowl.

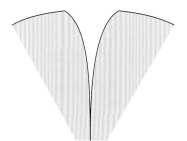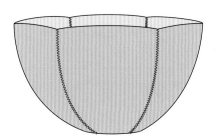

Use tapered darts for softly rounded bowls.

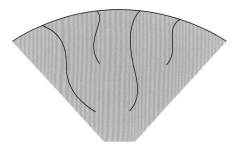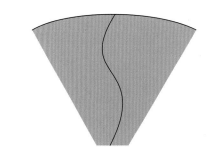

For uniquely shaped bowls, use secondary darts.

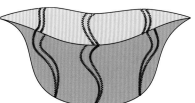

Curved darts add interest and shape to a bowl.

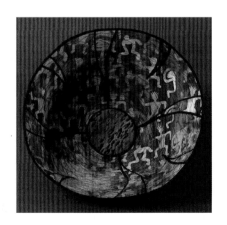

bowls

ROUND BOWL

This wonderful project is great for a novice to learn satin stitching and machine quilting. Get ready—sharp-looking curves ahead!

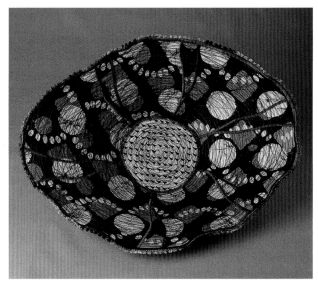

What You'll Need

- 2 fat quarters of complementary fabrics
- 5″ scraps for bases (*optional*)
- 1 yard of fusible web
- ½ yard of unwashed heavyweight canvas
- Thread to match or contrast with fabrics
- Round dinner plate
- Compass
- Basting spray
- Topstitch 90/16 needle
- Basic supplies (See Materials and Supplies, page 5.)

LAYERING

1. Stack the materials by placing the fabrics right sides together and folding the canvas and fusible web so there are 2 layers. Pin the layers. Place the stack on your cutting mat.

2. Set a round plate, bottom up, on top of the stack. Holding it firmly, use it as a guide to draw a circle. Use a compass to extend the diameter (see Making Circles, page 10), or draw the line freehand in pencil, 1″–2″ beyond the edge of the plate.

tip **As you cut, slide the plate around to keep the layers flat.**

3. Rotary cut along the extended circle, adding a small outward notch somewhere along the edge so you can easily realign the layers.

Rotary cut beyond the plate.

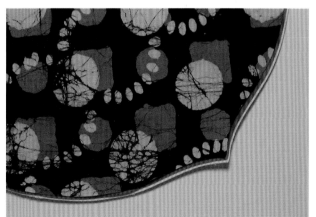
Cut a notch to help with realignment.

4. Remove the pins and align the circles of fabric, fusible web, and canvas, using the notches as a guide. Fuse the web to the fabric, then the fabric to the canvas. Temporarily adhere the canvas layers together with basting spray.

ADDING THE BASES

1. Apply fusible web to the back of 2 fabric and 2 canvas 5″ scraps.

2. Use a compass to draw a 4″ circle on the paper backing of the fusible web on just 1 of the canvas pieces. Cut this circle out with scissors.

3. Cut out 1 fabric base, making it ⅟₁₆″ larger all around than the canvas base.

4. Use a ruler to locate the center of the large textile sandwich. Fold the base into quarters, and lightly crease the point. Unfold, and insert a pin from the fabric side at the center point. Remove the paper backing, and insert the pin through the dot in the center of the textile sandwich. Keep the pin in place until you can smooth the canvas base out and press to fuse.

Center the canvas base on the textile sandwich.

5. Flip the textile sandwich. Peel the paper backing off the remaining 5″ scrap of fusible-backed canvas. Use basting spray to temporarily adhere it in place, checking that it's centered over the first base.

6. Using a slightly shortened stitch length, straight stitch around the first neatly cut base, keeping the stitches ⅟₁₆″ to the inside of the edge. Turn the textile sandwich over and trim away excess canvas beyond the stitches. Pull up on the fabric as you are trimming to get a nice close trim. Press to fuse the second canvas base in place.

> *tip* **A pair of double-curved appliqué scissors helps you get as close as possible to the stitching and produces a nice, smooth edge.**

Trim the second canvas base after stitching.

7. Repeat Steps 2–6 to apply the fabric bases. Satin stitch around the edge of the base. Your stitches should cover the edge of the base on both sides of the bowl.

QUILTING

1. Quilt the base. This holds the layers together and makes the base more stable. Use a straight-stitch design or consider free-motion quilting (page 11). End with a few lockstitches (page 9) at an edge or along previous stitches.

2. For the sides, set your machine to a slightly shorter straight stitch. Make lockstitches alongside the satin stitches around the base; then straight stitch in an ever-widening spiral toward the outer edge. Gently shift the textile sandwich back and forth as you sew to produce wavy stitching lines.

SHAPING

The steepness of your bowl's sides will depend on the number of darts and how much you overlap each dart. (See Creating Darts, page 12.)

1. For your first round bowl, mark 6 darts by inserting 6 pins spaced fairly evenly around the base and/or the edges of the sandwich.

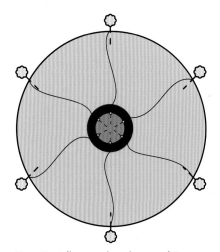

Note: Dart lines are imaginary only!

2. Using scissors, cut a gently curving line from 1 pin along the outer edge of your unshaped bowl to within about ¼″ of the base. Refer to the diagram, but cut only 1 curvy line. You'll be creating an overlap for this dart, not removing it, and you'll stitch along only 1 edge of the first dart before you cut the next dart.

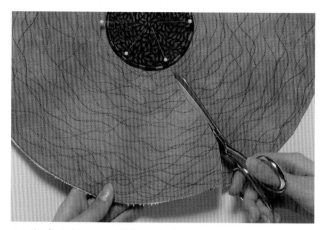

Cut the first dart; stop ¼″ from the base.

3. Set your sewing machine to a very open zigzag. Sew from the base toward the outer edge. Start sewing before the dart actually starts. (This eases the transition.) Sew along the dart, overlapping the cut edges slightly at the start, then increasingly to about 1″ at the outer edge. You may need to hold the dart together close to where you are sewing. Keep the overlap smooth and the zigzag stitch centered over the cut edge of the fabric.

As you stitch, increase the overlap.

4. Repeat Steps 2 and 3 until you have cut and zigzag stitched 1 side of each dart. If you like the bowl shape, satin stitch over the zigzag. If you don't, use a seam ripper to rip out the stitches of 1 or more darts and resew them.

5. Flip the bowl to the reverse side, and satin stitch along the other edge of the cut darts.

6. For a more finished look, satin stitch over all the darts a second time. Secure the beginning of each line of stitches with backstitches or lockstitches.

FINISHING

1. Using scissors, trim the outer edge of the bowl so none of the bare canvas is showing and the bowl edge has the shape you want.

2. Satin stitch around the rim twice. For a wavy rim, tug on the fabric as you stitch the edge. For the first round, use a medium-width stitch; for the second time around, use a slightly wider satin stitch.

3. End your stitching with a few lockstitches.

VARIATIONS

When you get a-*round* to trying something a little different, you'll find these techniques a cinch to do.

A. For a deeper bowl, add more darts, but cut them only half as long as the original darts. (*Round Bowl by Linda Johansen*)

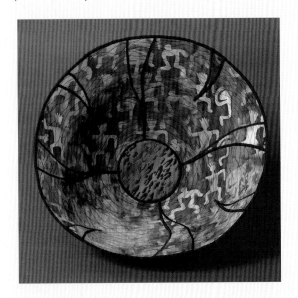

B. Take a rest from all that satin stitching and create a sawtooth edging (at right). (*Round Bowl by Linda Johansen*)

Tired of all the satin stitching? Try this technique for a unique finish to your bowl creation.

1. Cut a 12″ × 8″ piece of fabric.

2. Apply fusible web to the back of the fabric, remove the paper backing, and then cut it into 2″ squares. (You could also use a light coat of basting spray instead of the fusible web if you prefer.)

3. Work on an ironing surface protected with a nonstick pressing sheet. Place each small square along the edge of the bowl, so that 2 opposite points are along the edge. Overlap the squares by about ¾″, and when you get to the last square, tuck it under the first one.

Overlap small squares all around the edge.

4. Press the small squares in place. Flip the textile sandwich and tug a little on the squares as you press them in place on the second side.

5. Sew wavy lines around the edge to better secure the edges of the small squares. Use this opportunity to add more spirals around the bowl, because after you sew the darts you won't be able to add any more stitching.

Create either of two hexagonal shapes— one with straight edges, the other with pointed edges. In either case, choose fabrics that excite you, such as unexpected flannels or fun and funky prints.

What You'll Need

- 2 fat quarters of complementary fabrics
- 5″ scraps of accent fabrics for bases
- 1 yard of fusible web
- 1 package, or ½ yard, of Timtex for stabilizer

- Thread to match or contrast with fabrics
- Large sheet of newsprint paper for pattern
- Large clear quilter's rulers: rectangular ruler with marked 60° line and square ruler 12½″ or larger
- Basic supplies (See Materials and Supplies, page 5.)

MAKING THE PATTERNS

1. Using the square ruler, measure and cut a 10″ × 12″ rectangle of paper. Fold the paper lengthwise in half so that it measures 5″ × 12″, and place it on a cutting mat.

2. Align the 60° line of a rectangular quilter's ruler on the fold as shown. Cut along the long edge of the ruler.

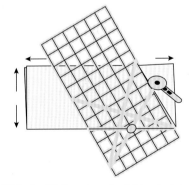

With the 60° line along the fold, cut along the long edge.

3. Unfold the paper, and then make cuts 10″ from each of the edges you just cut.

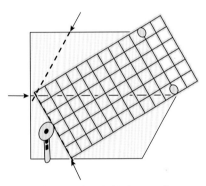

Make the second and third cuts 10″ away from the first cut.

4. For the base pattern, start with a 3″ × 5″ piece of paper or index card. Referring to Steps 2 and 3, fold it lengthwise in half, cut a 60° angle, and then make cuts so the finished hexagon measures 3″ from one side to the other.

LAYERING

1. Place the paper pattern for the 10″ hexagon on Timtex, securing it with tape. Align a rotary ruler with each side of the hexagon pattern, and rotary cut a Timtex hexagon.

2. Stack 2 fabrics and 2 layers of fusible web. Place the 10″ Timtex hexagon on top of the stack, and rotary cut ½″ larger than the Timtex all around.

3. Press fusible web to the wrong side of each fabric hexagon. Center 1 large fusible-backed piece of fabric on the Timtex, and press to fuse. Use a rotary cutter and ruler to trim each side even with the Timtex. Fuse fabric to the other side of the Timtex, and trim the edges.

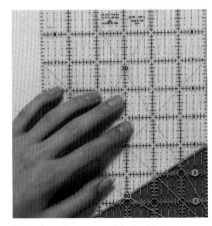

Trim the edges even with the Timtex.

ADDING THE BASES

1. Apply fusible web to the wrong side of 2 pieces of fabric, each about 5" square. Cut out 2 bases, using the 3" hexagon paper pattern.

2. Use a ruler to draw 1 set of lines—*either* for Option A *or* for Option B. Work on either side of the textile sandwich, using any marking tool that will show up.

Option A:
Straight Edges from Dart to Dart

Using a ruler, draw 3 guidelines, each connecting opposite corners and crossing the center of the textile sandwich.

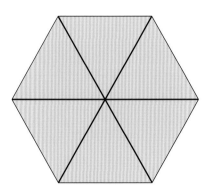

Guidelines for Option A

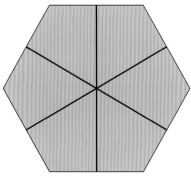

Guidelines for Option B

Option B:
Pointed Edges between Darts

Measure and mark the midpoint of each edge of the hexagonal textile sandwich. Using a ruler, draw 3 guidelines, each connecting opposite midpoints and crossing the center of the textile sandwich.

3. With either option, place a 3" hexagon base with each corner on a line. Press to fuse it in place.

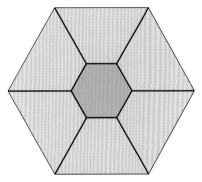

Positioning the base for Option A

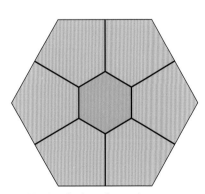

Positioning the base for Option B

4. Straight stitch just outside the edges of the base. Sew as close as possible to the base, but not on it. Flip the textile sandwich to the other side, and position the second fusible-backed fabric hexagon inside the stitching. Press to fuse this piece in place.

5. Use some scraps similar to the textile sandwich to check your stitches and tension before you begin stitching on the bowl. Using a medium-width satin stitch, sew around the edge of the base once or twice, until it looks finished to you. As you sew, keep the center of the satin stitch along the edge of the base.

SHAPING

1. Mark points at the edge of the textile sandwich, ½" to either side of each guideline you marked across the center of the sandwich.

2. Connect these marks to a point ⅛" from the corner of the base. Draw in all the darts before you begin to cut them out and stitch them.

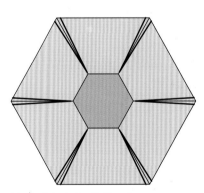

Marked darts for Option A

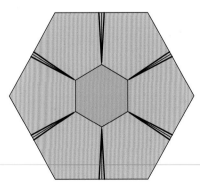

Marked darts for Option B

3. Cut along the 2 marked lines, and remove 1 dart only. Sharp scissors really help here!

4. Set your machine for a medium satin stitch, and use the cutout dart piece as a scrap to check the stitches and tension. Place the needle of your machine exactly at 1 corner of the base, with the cutout dart in front of the needle. Sew a few satin stitches, and then backstitch to anchor the thread.

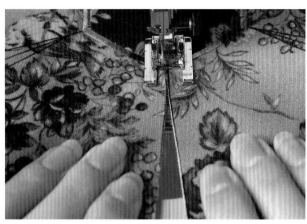

Begin stitching the dart at the base.

5. Continue satin stitching toward the edge of the textile sandwich. As you sew, pull the edges of the dart together in front of the needle, so the zigzag stitch catches both edges equally. Work slowly—if you try to pull the whole dart together when you start, you'll have puckering at the base of the dart. Stop when you reach the edge, and don't backstitch, because satin stitching along the edge will secure these threads later.

6. Cut and stitch the remaining 5 darts the same way. For a more finished look, go over each dart again, using a slightly wider satin stitch.

FINISHING

1. If necessary, use small, sharp scissors to trim the textile sandwich on either side of the dart so that the edges meet perfectly at the dart.

2. Satin stitch around the edge of the bowl, using the same setting. You want the right side of the satin stitch to consistently fall just beyond the edge of the fabric. Make a second round using a slightly wider satin stitch. Finish off with lockstitches.

VARIATIONS

Novelty fabrics and conversation prints will inspire you to make a different version of this bowl for each season of the year.

A. The pointy version of this design brings pointy-petaled poinsettias and Christmas to mind, inspiring a bowl for everyone on your gift list. *(Hexagon Bowl by Linda Johansen)*

B. Symbolize the freshness of spring with a floral or barnyard print. This bowl starts from a 12″ circle, but the rest of the process is the same. *(Hexagon Bowl by Linda Johansen)*

OCTAGON BOWL

Don't let the elegant look fool you—the eight darts cut along the circle base lead effortlessly to that rich, ribbed texture and graceful, scalloped edge.

LAYERING

1. Use a round plate, and a compass if necessary, to cut a 13"-diameter circle from Timtex. (Refer to Making Circles, page 10, and Round Bowl, Step 3, page 15, as needed.)

2. Using the Timtex as a pattern, cut out circles ½" larger all around: 1 from each fabric, and 2 from fusible web. Press a fusible web circle to the wrong side of each fabric circle.

3. Remove the paper backing from both large fabric circles. Protect your ironing surface with a pressing sheet. Fuse 1 fabric circle to the Timtex. Let cool; then trim the edges even with the Timtex. Repeat to fuse a fabric circle to the other side, and trim the edges even.

MARKING 8 DIVISION LINES

1. Using a long quilter's ruler with a marked 45°, locate the exact center of the textile sandwich, and mark with a dot.

2. Draw a line across the exact center of the circle. Draw a second line at a 90° angle to the first.

3. Draw a third line at a 45° angle to 1 of the first 2 lines. Draw a fourth line at a 90° angle to the last line drawn. You should have 8 even sections marked.

ADDING THE BASES

1. Apply fusible web to the wrong side of 2 pieces (or scraps) of fabric, each at least 4½" square. On the paper backing of 1 of the pieces, draw a 3½" circle with a compass. Cut it out with scissors; don't mark or cut the second piece yet.

2. To find the center of the 3½" base, fold it into quarters with the paper backing on the inside, and lightly crease the point. Unfold, and insert a pin up through the circle, from the fabric side, at the center point. Remove the paper backing from the fusible web.

3. Insert the pin into the center of the textile sandwich where all the lines cross. Press to fuse the base in place.

Center the base on the textile sandwich.

4. Peel away the paper from the second fabric scrap and center it on the reverse side of the textile sandwich. Peek under the sandwich to make sure it covers the same area that the first base occupies. Apply basting spray to temporarily hold it in place.

5. Using a slightly shortened stitch length, straight stitch around the smaller base, keeping stitches ¹⁄₁₆" to the inside of the edge. Flip the textile sandwich and trim away the excess fabric beyond the stitches.

> *tip* **Double-curved appliqué scissors make close trimming a cinch to do.**

6. Press to fuse the second base in place. Check your stitches and tension on a scrap of layered materials, and then sew a medium-width satin stitch around the edge of the base.

Satin stitch around the base.

> *tip* **This bowl does not need any stitching to firm up the base, but consider adding some decorative quilting anyway!**

MARKING AND CUTTING DARTS

1. Photocopy dart patterns A and B (below) at 175%. From the enlarged copies, make templates by cutting them out from paper or template plastic, and mark the centerline with a ruler.

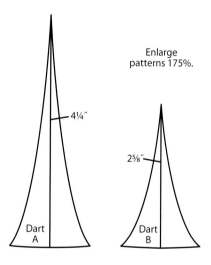

Enlarge patterns 175%.

4¼"

2⅝"

Dart A

Dart B

2. Place the centerline of 1 template on a marked division line, matching the outer edges. Trace along both long edges of the template. Repeat this step around the circle, alternating templates A and B for long and short darts. Mark all the darts before cutting and sewing.

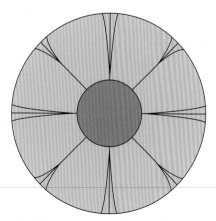

Mark the darts, alternating templates A and B.

SHAPING

1. Cut along the 2 marked lines of a long A dart, and remove the dart. Cut with sharp scissors, and cut only 1 dart at a time just before you sew, so there's less opportunity for the fabric to fray.

Cut and stitch 1 dart at a time.

2. Use a medium-width satin stitch, and check your stitches and tension on a cutout dart. Place the needle of your machine exactly at the edge of the base, with the cut edges of an A dart in front of the needle. Sew a few stitches, backstitch to anchor the thread, and then continue toward the edge of the textile sandwich. As you sew, pull the edges of the dart together to meet just in front of the needle, and keep the zigzag stitch centered over both edges. Work slowly and carefully. If you try to pull the whole dart together when you start, you'll have puckering at the base of the dart.

3. The bowl will begin to curve a lot more as you get close to the rim. At this point, you will need to pull quite firmly. Continue stitching to the edge of the textile sandwich. No need to backstitch—satin stitching along the edge will take care of catching these threads later.

4. Next, satin stitch a shorter B dart. Again, begin sewing at the edge of the base, and sew along the entire marked line, as if you had cut it all the way to the base. In this way, cut and sew all the darts as you come to them. When that is done, go over each dart a second time, using a slightly wider satin stitch. Backstitch at the beginning to anchor the thread.

Sew along the entire marked line of a B dart.

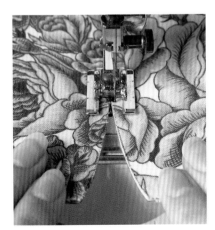

Bring the cut edges of the dart together as you stitch.

FINISHING

1. The edges of your bowl should form gentle, even scallops. If they don't, use a pair of sharp scissors to carefully trim the high edge to meet the lower one.

2. Sew around the edge of the bowl with a medium-width satin stitch. You want the right side of the satin stitch to consistently fall just beyond the edge of the fabric. Pivot at each dart to make a crisp angle.

3. Repeat, using a slightly wider satin stitch. Finish off with lockstitches.

 For a very different bowl, mark and cut straight darts.

VARIATIONS

The graceful lines of this bowl enable you to dress it up or down.

A. For a feminine, garden-party look, choose a floral print. Trace around the edge of a teacup to make the scallops rounder and deeper. *(Garden Party Bowl by Linda Johansen)*

B. If you're after a contemporary, angular shape, use a ruler to draw the darts, straightening the curves of the templates. *(Contemporary Bowl by Linda Johansen)*

PIECED BOWL

This is a great way to use up your scraps of fabric and stiff interfacing. Or you can simply take two fat quarters and play with some geometric shapes.

What You'll Need

- 2 fat quarters of fabric (or scraps)

- ½ yard of stiff interfacing (or scraps)

- 1 yard of fusible web (not needed if using fast2fuse)

- 1 yard of cording

- Thread to match or contrast with fabrics

- Equilateral 60° triangle ruler, regular rotary ruler with marked 60° angle, or template made from triangle pattern (page 29)

- Basic supplies (See Materials and Supplies, page 5.)

CUTTING

1. Cut 2 pieces of stiff interfacing: 1 piece 4½″ × 4½″ and 1 piece 11″ × 11″.

2. Cut 2 pieces 4½″ × 4½″ and 2 pieces 11″ × 11″ of fabric—1 piece for each side.

3. Repeat Step 2 for fusible web, if needed.

LAYERING

1. Iron the fusible web to the wrong side of the fabrics first; then fuse 1 piece of fabric to each side of the interfacing pieces. If using fast2fuse, just iron the fabric to each side of the fast2fuse.

2. Trim the small piece to 4″ × 4″ square.

3. For the triangles, cut the larger piece into 3½″ strips, and use a 60° triangle ruler or make a template from the pattern (page 29) to cut the strips into 12 triangles 3½″ high.

tip **Use up those scraps; fuse fabric to pieces of stiff interfacing slightly larger than the 3½″ triangle, and then cut the triangles.**

tip **If you don't have a triangular ruler, use the 60° mark on your regular rotary ruler. Just lay the 60° mark of the ruler on the edge of the 3½″ strip and cut the angle for the triangle.**

SHAPING

1. Sew 4 triangle pieces to the square base with a wide zigzag stitch (4.0 or wider). Butt the edges together, and center the stitching to catch an equal amount of each edge.

2. Sew the remaining 8 triangles onto the first 4 with the same zigzag stitch. The piece is still flat at this point.

Cut the 3½″ strips into equilateral triangles.

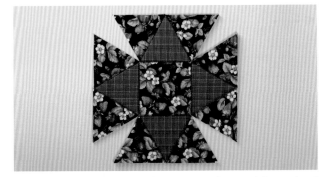

Sew the first 4 triangles to the base. Sew on the remaining 8 triangles.

3. Satin stitch over all the zigzagged joinings.

4. Satin stitch the corners. Start in the existing satin stitching, backstitch a few stitches to hold the thread ends, and gradually pull the sides together as you sew up them. Pulling together too quickly will give you lumps at the start of the stitching.

Gently pull together the sides as you sew.

tip **If your needle is punching the stiff interfacing or fabric threads through on the back side, change to a smaller needle. I sometimes use a sharps 70/10.**

5. Satin stitch over the seams again if you think the bowl needs it.

FINISHING

1. Trim the edges even, as needed.

2. Zigzag the cording on (page 9), and then satin stitch around the outer edge. Add a second layer of satin stitching if desired.

There are so many ways to use up scraps. Have fun with these variations and use the technique to make up some of your own.

A. Rather than satin stitch over the cording, let the zigzag stitch be an embellishment! Here black zigzag stitching over white cording is the perfect complement to this bowl. *(Black-and-White Pieced Bowl by Linda Johansen)*

B. Use four small triangles instead of a large one and zigzag the triangles together for a bowl with stiffer edges and sharper corners. *(Four Small Tri-Base Bowl by Linda Johansen)*

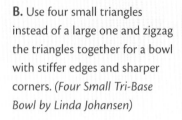

3½˝

Pieced Bowl Triangle
Cut 12.

FLUTED BOWL

Graceful, flowing, and formal, a Fluted Bowl can decorate your table all by itself. Add a candle or vase of flowers in it, and you have a lovely centerpiece. This shape works beautifully with floral fabrics.

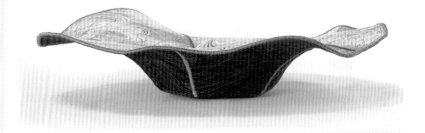

What You'll Need

- 2 fat quarters of fabric
- ½ yard of unwashed heavyweight canvas, denim, or duck fabric
- 1 yard of fusible web
- 1½ yards of cording
- Temporary adhesive basting spray
- Topstitch 80/12 or 90/16 needle
- Template material (*optional*)
- Pattern (page 33)
- Basic supplies (See Materials and Supplies, page 5.)

LAYERING

1. Cut 2 layers each of fabric, canvas, and fusible web to a circle approximately 16″ in diameter. Refer to Making Circles (page 10) as necessary.

2. Iron a piece of fusible web to the back of each circle of fabric, and then fuse a fabric circle to each canvas circle.

ADDING THE BASES

1. Cut 2 canvas 4″ circles for the base. (Refer to Making Circles, page 10, as necessary.)

2. Lightly spray temporary adhesive on the canvas side of 1 layer of your sandwich.

3. Center a 4″ canvas base on the sticky canvas. Before you spray, you can carefully measure to center or just eyeball it.

4. Lightly spray this 4″ circle, and put the second one on top of it.

5. Lay the other 16″ circle on top, canvas side down, fabric side up. If it doesn't hold, turn it over and lightly spray the canvas side. Press the canvas sides together firmly with your hands.

QUILTING

Your quilting of the whole sandwich is enough if you don't want the stitching as a design element accentuating the base.

1. Mark an indentation at the edge of the base on 1 side by firmly pressing around it with your fingernail or a blunt point, such as a pen with the ink cartridge retracted. (Be sure to clean the point of the pen before using it.) Use a quilt marking pencil or chalk if you can't see the indentations.

2. Sew around the circle on this indented mark with a straight stitch to mark the base clearly.

3. Cover the straight stitch with a 4.0-width satin stitch. Anchor your stitches with a few short-length straight stitches at the end, right beside the satin stitch.

> *tip* **Lower the pressure on the presser foot for sewing on the base, if your sewing machine has that option.**

4. Sew within the base to anchor the layers together.

> *tip* **Sew the entire surface with the same stitches—stippling or following the fabric pattern without accenting the base.**

5. Shorten your straight stitch (2.0 length). Begin stitching to the right of the base. Anchor your stitching with a few short stitches just outside the satin stitching. Turn the sandwich counterclockwise while sewing so that the amount of fabric under the arm of your machine becomes less as you sew. (See Quilting, Step 1, page 16.)

6. Stitch the sides with an ever-widening wavy spiral or stippling, or just follow lines in the fabric. To make waves, hold the left edge with your hand and gently guide the edge back and forth as you sew around. Cross lines randomly as you sew. The surface works best with lots of stitching to hold the layers together when you cut darts.

SHAPING

1. Mark the placement of 5 darts by inserting 5 pins spaced fairly evenly around the base of the sandwich.

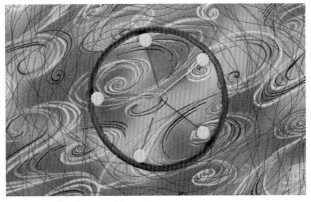

Insert pins evenly spaced for 5 darts.

2. Using a marker, trace 5 darts using the pattern (page 33). Place the dart point ⅛″–¼″ from the edge of the base satin stitching.

Mark the darts.

3. Cut the first dart on the marked lines and remove the dart's center.

Cut the first dart.

4. Set your machine for a wide (4.5 or 5) zigzag stitch. Test your stitching on scraps of the canvas and fabric.

5. Begin sewing near the edge of the base, just before the dart begins. Gently and *firmly* pull the edges together to meet just ahead of the needle. It does take some muscle because the edges come up steeply at first.

Firmly pull the edges together as you sew.

6. As you sew the dart, pull outward so that the dart edges just meet. The excess fabric is what causes the edge to ripple so nicely!

7. Trim the thread ends at the base after each line of stitching so they don't get caught in the next darts.

8. Repeat this process until you have cut and stitched each dart.

9. Go over each dart with a satin stitch. Remember to backstitch a few stitches to the edge of the base when you begin sewing up the dart. This will lock your stitches.

FINISHING

1. Trim the outer edge of the bowl.

2. Zigzag the cording on (page 9), and then satin stitch around the outer edge. For a smoother finished look, add a second layer of satin stitching.

(page 9)

VARIATIONS

Try changing the shape of the sandwich, or the shape of the darts, or even adding a center for some interesting and exciting variations. Add a contrasting center to carry through on a theme.

A. Canvas can go square, too! (*Square Fluted Bowl by Alex Vincent*)

B. You can change the shape of the darts, still butting them together, and then appliqué stones and add decorative stitching, as I did for this commissioned piece. (*Bowl with Appliquéd Stones and Decorative Stitching by Linda Johansen, courtesy of Loreen Olufson*)

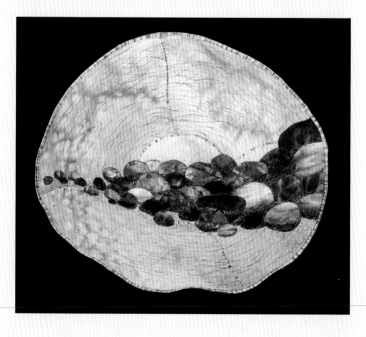

Base

Fluted Bowl Dart

Edge

SUNFLOWER BOWL

Spread some sunshine around your home with a few of these sunny faces.

What You'll Need

- 2 fat quarters of "sunny" fabrics
- 2 scraps, approximately 4" square, of fabric for flower center
- ½ yard of canvas, denim, or duck fabric
- 1 yard of fusible web
- 1¼ yards of cording
- Thread to contrast with flower fabric
- Temporary adhesive basting spray
- Freezer paper (6" × 15")
- Topstitch 90/16 needle
- Pattern (page 38)
- Basic supplies (See Materials and Supplies, page 5.)

LAYERING

1. Apply fusible web to the wrong side of 2 fabric squares 13" × 13". Peel the paper backing from the fabric squares, and fuse each of them to a 13" square of canvas.

2. Draw a 12" circle on each of the fused squares, and cut the circles out using scissors or a large rotary cutter. Refer to Making Circles (page 10) as necessary.

> *tip* Mark a circle, stack the layers, put a dinner plate upside down to firmly hold the sandwich, press firmly with a rotary cutter, and cut both pieces at the same time.

3. Spray the canvas side of a circle with a temporary spray adhesive.

> *tip* Remember to take off the fusible web before stitching the bases.

4. Layer the circles on a flat surface with canvas sides together, and press firmly with your hand. If the layers do not hold together, try spraying both sides lightly. Overspraying will gum up your needle when you sew the sides.

ADDING THE BASES

1. Apply fusible web to 2 canvas 4" scraps.

2. Apply fusible web to the back of 2 scraps of fabric, at least 4" square. They must be larger than the canvas scraps. These fabrics will be the center of your "flower" and the base of the bowl.

3. Freehand cut a circle about 3"–3½" from 1 piece of canvas, or use a school compass or circle cutter to make the circle. (Refer to Making Circles, page 10, as necessary.) Make this circle about ¼" smaller around than you want the base.

4. Lay a piece of the base fabric over the cut canvas piece, and cut it 1/16" larger all around than the canvas base. This piece should be the size you want the center. If you cut these freehand, place a pin in the same direction on each of them so that you can match the shape when they get fused. Keep uncut 1 fabric and 1 canvas scrap with fusible on the back.

5. Place the canvas circle in the center of the bowl sandwich. Eyeball it—flowers aren't perfect! Fuse in place. Leave in the directional pin.

Match the direction of the pins on the cut canvas and fabric bases.

6. Center the second, untrimmed canvas scrap on the other side of the fabric sandwich. Check to be sure that it is centered over the first base.

7. With the untrimmed scrap on the bottom, straight stitch around the cutout base. Sew about 1/16" inside the edge.

8. Turn the sandwich over, and trim away the canvas that extends outside the stitching. Use your double-curved, duck-billed scissors, and pull up on the fabric as you are trimming. This will give you a nice close trim, and the edges of the bases will line up perfectly.

Pull up on the edge as you cut to a get a close trim.

9. Fuse the second canvas base in place.

10. Fuse the cut fabric base over the first canvas base, matching the directional pins or centering it.

11. Sew and trim the fabric bases the same way you did the canvas bases. Iron the fabrics to be sure the bases are well fused.

12. Stitch within the base to stabilize all the layers. A double-zigzag mending stitch works well for the base to make it really look like sunflower seeds. Begin stitching around the outer edge of the base, and sew more slowly and turn the sandwich faster as you get toward the center.

13. Satin stitch around the edge of the base using a 4.0 stitch width. Center the stitch between the edge of the base and the stitching line just inside the edge so your stitches will be sure to cover the edge of the base on the reverse side.

QUILTING

Use a decorative thread, and sew around the bowl with a wavy spiral. Start to the right of the center, and sew with the sandwich moving counterclockwise. This keeps the bulk of the sandwich to the left of the sewing machine arm rather than under it.

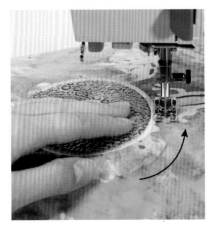

Sew so that the sandwich moves counterclockwise.

SHAPING

1. Using the pattern (page 38), trace the petal, with the dart, onto freezer paper. Pin together 6 layers of freezer paper, and cut out 6 petals, including the dart on each side. While the layers are still pinned together, mark the darts through all the layers by stitching along the petal dart lines with an old needle and no thread in your machine.

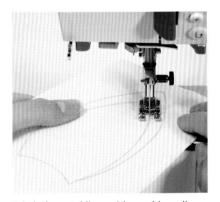

Stitch the petal lines with an old needle and no thread.

2. Arrange the freezer-paper petals onto the sandwich. There should be about 1/4" between the petals at the base of the bowl. Restack and pin the petals and trim slightly if necessary. The petal points may extend a bit beyond the edge of the sandwich. This is okay. Iron the petals on the sandwich.

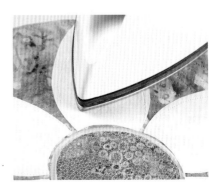

Press the freezer-paper petals onto the sandwich.

3. Cut along the outside dart edges on each side of the petal. Then, cut straight in from the edge to the tip of the petal.

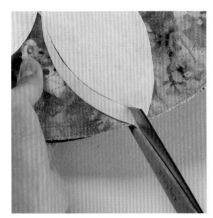

Cut straight in from the edge to the tip of the petal.

4. Cut along the inside edge of the dart, and remove the dart. Do this on both sides of 1 petal. Remove the freezer paper from the petal you just cut.

Cut along the inside perforated edge of the dart.

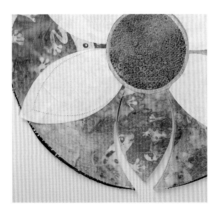

Darts for 1 petal cut

5. Use a zigzag stitch to sew 1 side of the petal, gently pulling the edges together. The edge of the sandwich will stick out farther than the end of the petal. Leave it for now.

6. Zigzag up the second side of the petal. Stop about an inch before you get to the top of the petal.

7. Overlap the points and trim them even. Then trim just a tiny bit more off 1 side so the bowl will continue to round up.

Overlap the points and trim them.

8. Finish sewing the dart.

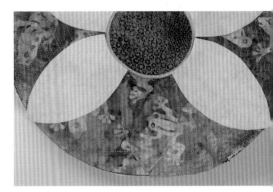

A petal with darts stitched

9. Trim the thread ends at the base after stitching each petal, so they don't get caught in the next dart.

10. Repeat this process until you have cut and stitched a dart on each side of each petal.

11. Make any shape adjustments you want, and then sew over each dart line with a satin stitch.

FINISHING

1. Trim the edge so no canvas shows. Be sure to check from both sides.

2. Add the cording (page 9) as you satin stitch around the outer edge. Add a second layer of satin stitching if desired.

3. Embellish as you wish!

> *tip* **Try this one with fast2fuse. Eliminate the surface quilting, and add an extra layer of fast2fuse under the fabric of the base on one side of the sandwich. Fuse the fabric to the fast2fuse, and then use steam and press firmly to adhere the extra base piece.**

VARIATIONS

Fun in the sun—make your own bouquet of sunflowers for the summer or winter. By changing the colors and petal shapes, you can change the mood of this bowl and still keep it cheery and uplifting.

A. Trim the background, shape it a bit, fuse another color over it, and you have a flower with double the petals. *(Blue Two-Color Bowl by Sidnee Snell)*

B. Round the petals and the background for a soft summer flower. *(Round Petal Edges by Libby Ankarberg)*

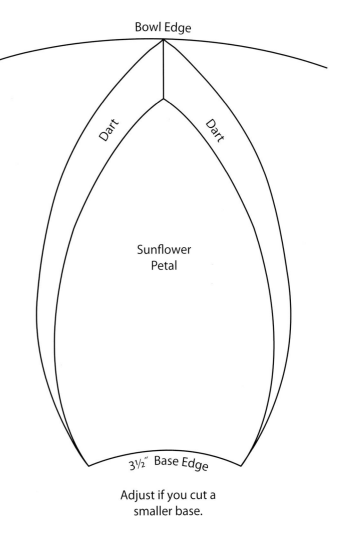

Bowl Edge

Dart   Dart

Sunflower
Petal

3½″ Base Edge

Adjust if you cut a
smaller base.

boxes

SQUARE BOX

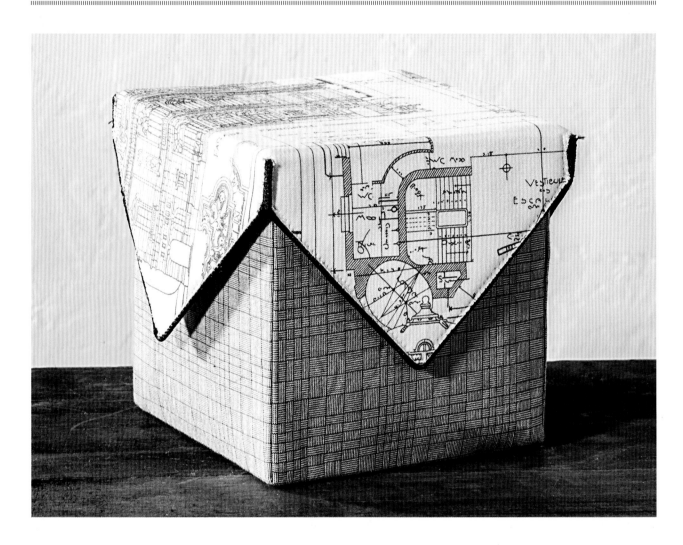

Go ahead—be square! You will think up so many variations for this one, you'll never get boxed in.

What You'll Need

- Fabric: 1 fat quarter each of 2 fabrics for 3″ or 4″ box; ½ yard each of 2 fabrics for 5″ box

- Stiff interfacing: ¼ yard for 3″ or 4″ box; ⅓ yard for 5″ box

- Fusible web: ⅝ yard for 3″ box; 1 yard for 4″ box; 1½ yards for 5″ box

- Basic supplies (See Materials and Supplies, page 5.)

CUTTING

Square 3″ Box

From stiff interfacing: Cut 7 squares 3″ × 3″ (5 for the box, 2 for the lid flaps) and 1 square 3½″ × 3½″ (for the lid base).

For lid flaps: Use 2 of the 3″ × 3″ stiff interfacing squares. Following the instructions in Lid Construction (page 44), trim off the corners 1¾″ out from the centerline, so the measurement from trimmed corner to trimmed corner is 3½″ (lid-base width).

From both fabrics: Cut 1 square 10″ × 10″ for the box and 1 square 7″ × 7″ for the lid. Cut 2 of each size square from the fusible web.

Square 4″ Box

From stiff interfacing: Cut 7 squares 4″ × 4″ (5 for the box, 2 for the lid flaps) and 1 square 4½″ × 4½″ (for the lid base).

For lid flaps: Use 2 of the 4″ × 4″ stiff interfacing squares. Following the instructions in Lid Construction (page 44), trim off the corners. Cut 2¼″ out from the drawn line, parallel with it, to match the lid-base width of 4½″.

From both fabrics: Cut 1 square 12½″ × 12½″ for the box and 1 square 8″ × 8″ for the lid. Cut 2 of each size square from the fusible web.

Square 5″ Box

From stiff interfacing: Cut 7 squares 5″ × 5″ (5 for the box, 2 for the lid flaps) and 1 square 5½″ × 5½″ (for the lid base).

For lid flaps: Use 2 of the 5″ × 5″ squares. Following the instructions in Lid Construction (page 44), trim off the corners 2¾″ out from the drawn line to match the lid-base width of 5½″.

From both fabrics: Cut 1 square 16″ × 16″ for the box and 1 square 10″ × 10″ for the lid. Cut 2 of each size square from the fusible web.

BOX CONSTRUCTION

LAYERING

1. Using the shapes you cut for the specific box you wish to make, use white thread and wide, long zigzag stitches to sew the base and side squares of stiff interfacing together, 1 stitch catching each piece of stiff interfacing. Hold the pieces apart slightly as you sew. (The examples use orange thread to make the pieces easier to see.)

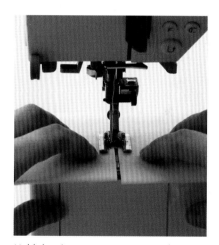

Hold the pieces apart as you sew them together.

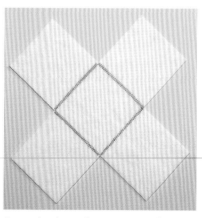

Square box base pieces sewn together

2. Using the 2 fabric and 2 fusible web squares you cut for your specific box size, fuse the web to the wrong sides of the fabric pieces.

3. Lightly fuse 1 layer of fabric to the stiff interfacing you assembled in Step 1. Be sure your ironing board protective sheet is underneath the fabric and fusible when you do this.

 Press from the center out so you don't roll the edges of the fused fabric.

4. Turn the piece over and trim the fabric to the outer edges of the stiff interfacing, leaving the corners square.

The fabric is ready to be trimmed.

5. Lay the second piece of fusible-backed fabric on the stiff interfacing side of the sandwich, fusible side down. Make sure it is very flat, with no wrinkles underneath. Iron the fabric onto the sandwich. Be sure to fuse the fabrics well in the corners. Iron right up to the stiff interfacing.

6. Trim the second piece of fabric even with the first piece.

SEWING THE CORNERS

1. Fold diagonally so the 2 adjacent sides of the sandwich meet with the box's interior fabrics together.

2. Match the edges of the stiff interfacing, and put a pin in the excess corner fabric.

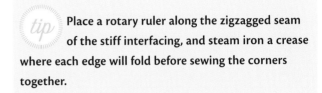 **Place a rotary ruler along the zigzagged seam of the stiff interfacing, and steam iron a crease where each edge will fold before sewing the corners together.**

3. Using a straight stitch, sew as close as you can along the edge of the stiff interfacing. Backstitch at the start. End the sewing about ⅛" from the corner and backstitch. If you stop stitching before the bottom corner, the stitching will be hidden!

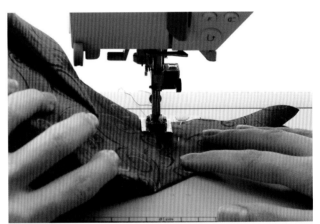

Sew the corner.

4. Continue folding and sewing the corners in the same way.

 Sew the corner seams with a shortened stitch length, trim the corners off, and turn the box inside out for a finished, nonreversible box.

FINISHING THE CORNERS

1. Iron a crease in the center of the fold on each corner.

2. Bring the crease to the corner of the box, and flatten the excess fabric along the sides of the box.

3. Pin the excess fabric to the box, keeping the pins below the edge. Repeat this on each corner.

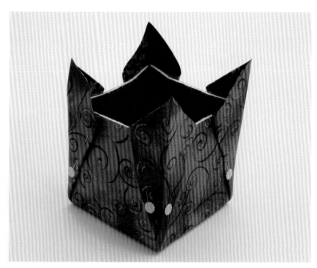

Pin the excess fabric to the sides. (Pins are below the edge!)

 tip **Fold two corners over each other on opposite sides for a different look.**

4. Steam press the corners flat against the box.

5. Trim the fabric even with the top edge of the box. Use your double-curved, duck-billed appliqué scissors for an easy, clean, and even edge.

Trim the corners.

6. Fit the box over the open arm of your machine. With the cording right next to the edge of the box, zigzag it on around the edge. See Using Cording (page 9).

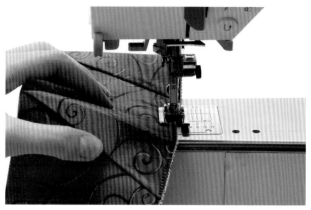

Sew the cording with the box over the arm of the sewing machine.

7. Sew around the top edge with a medium-width satin stitch. Be sure the stitch is wide enough to cover the cording and catch the edge of the box. Sew around the box again using a slightly wider satin stitch the second time around.

 tip **Use a marker to cover any threads or cording that are still showing.**

SHAPING

Set the box open-side down on your ironing board and steam press the sides and bottom flat. Don't press too hard!

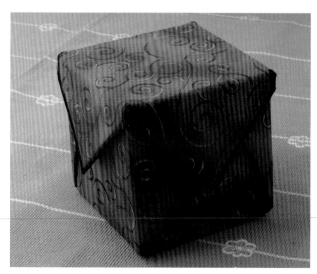

Steam the base. Using wood as a filler makes it easier.

LID CONSTRUCTION

CUTTING

1. Draw lines across each lid side square from corner to corner. Position the piece on your cutting mat so the lines form a plus sign (pencil lines in the photo below).

2. Cut off 2 corners to give the lid a snug fit on the box. The width of the piece after you trim the corners will be the same width as the lid base. Place your ruler along the horizontal line, using the vertical line as the centerline of your measurement. Mark the corner trimming lines. Cut off the corners parallel to the vertical line. Repeat this on the remaining side square lid pieces.

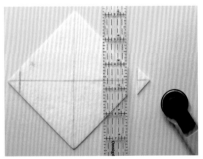

Draw 2 lines corner to corner. Nip the ends off the sides.

3. Cut both lid side squares in half along the horizontal line (through the clipped corners).

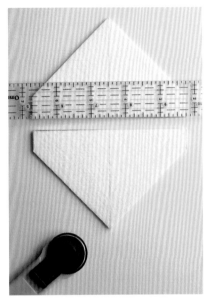

Cut on the horizontal line, trimmed edge to trimmed edge.

4. Sew these side pieces to the lid base with a loose zigzag stitch as you did for the box, holding them apart a bit as you sew.

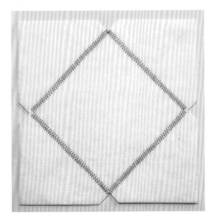

Lid base with the side flaps sewn on

5. Cut 2 pieces of fabric and 2 pieces of fusible web ½" larger all around.

LAYERING

1. Fuse a piece of web to the wrong side of each piece of fabric.

2. Fuse 1 piece of fabric to the assembled lid with stiff interfacing.

3. Trim the edges to match the shape of the stiff interfacing, including the little notch in the center of each side.

4. Turn the sandwich over and fuse the other piece of fabric to the stiff interfacing.

5. Trim the edges.

Trim the lid along the stiff interfacing. Here, the second fabric is fused on and 1 edge is trimmed, including the notch.

SEWING THE EDGES

1. Zigzag cording onto the perimeter of the flat lid shape. See Using Cording (page 9).

2. Satin stitch twice around the edges of the whole top while it is still flat. Use the same satin stitch widths you used on the edge of the box. Check the back side before sewing the second time around to make sure the first stitches caught all the fabric and completely covered the edge. Don't sew around the inner corners of the notches on the side. (Sew inside the notches, just not the inside corner of each notch.)

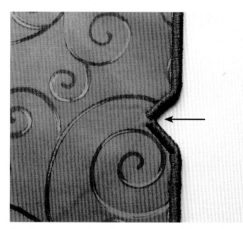

Don't sew around the inner corners of the notches.

SHAPING

1. Fold the corners of the lid in to the center and press them with steam so they retain some angle.

2. The notches that become the lid corners can be sewn together by hand or machine. Fold the lid to match the corners. Sew them together with a very narrow, short-length zigzag stitch very close to the outer edge. Repeat this for each corner. Remember, you can scrunch it to get it under the needle!

3. Steam the flaps in a bit more as necessary if they flare out.

> *tip* **Set the top on the box and steam press the top flat. Press gently so you don't distort the box shape.**

Now comes the hard part—figuring out what to put in it and who to give it to! Mix and match and make the boxes your own by trying some of these variations:

A. Fuse squares of a complementary fabric to the corners before stitching them closed. *(Square Box by Sidnee Snell)*

B. Round the lid flaps and add some decorative stitching before sewing the corners of the lid. *(Square Box by Sidnee Snell)*

HEXAGON BOX

These boxes can charm the jewelry right out of your ears or the cards right off the table! And they make great containers for any number of things you don't want to lose.

What You'll Need

- Fabric: 1 fat quarter each of 2 fabrics for small box; ½ yard each of 2 fabrics for large box

- Stiff interfacing: ½ yard for small or large box

- Fusible web: 1½ yards for small box; 2 yards for large box

- Patterns (page 48)

- Basic supplies (See Materials and Supplies, page 5.)

CUTTING

Small Hexagon Box

From stiff interfacing: Cut 6 squares 2⅝″ × 2⅝″ for the box sides. Using the patterns, cut 1 small box base (side edges will measure 2⅝″), 1 small lid base (side edges will measure 3″), and 6 small lid flaps.

Set the sewn stiff interfacing box (or lid) on top of 2 layers of fabric and 2 layers of fusible web. Cut ½″ outside the straight edges. Be sure to leave fabric and fusible for the corners of the box.

Large Hexagon Box

From stiff interfacing: Cut 6 squares 3¾″ × 3¾″ for the box sides. Using the patterns, cut 1 large box base (side edges will measure 3¾″), 1 large lid base (side edges will measure 4⅛″), and 6 large lid flaps.

Set the sewn stiff interfacing box (or lid) on top of 2 layers of fabric and 2 layers of fusible web. Cut ½″ outside the straight edges. Be sure to leave fabric and fusible for the corners of the box.

CONSTRUCTION

Using the pieces you cut for the size of box you wish to make, follow the Square Box instructions for Box Construction (page 41) and Lid Construction (page 44) to make your Hexagon Box.

Sew the stiff interfacing together for the Hexagon Box, fuse to the fabric, and trim the edges (4 edges trimmed).

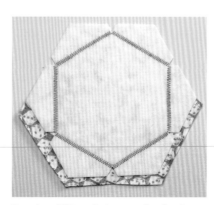

Sew the stiff interfacing together for the Hexagon Box lid, fuse to the fabric, and trim the edges and notches (3 edges trimmed).

VARIATIONS

These delicate shaped boxes can store everyday items or special treasures. Be sure to make one just the right size for your own unique needs.

A. Curve the lid flaps in and out and add some beads for a unique gift box. *(Hexagon Box by Kim Campbell)*

B. Fuse fabric to stiff interfacing cut the right size, and you can make some great divisions to keep your treasures separated. *(Hexagon Box by Sidnee Snell)*

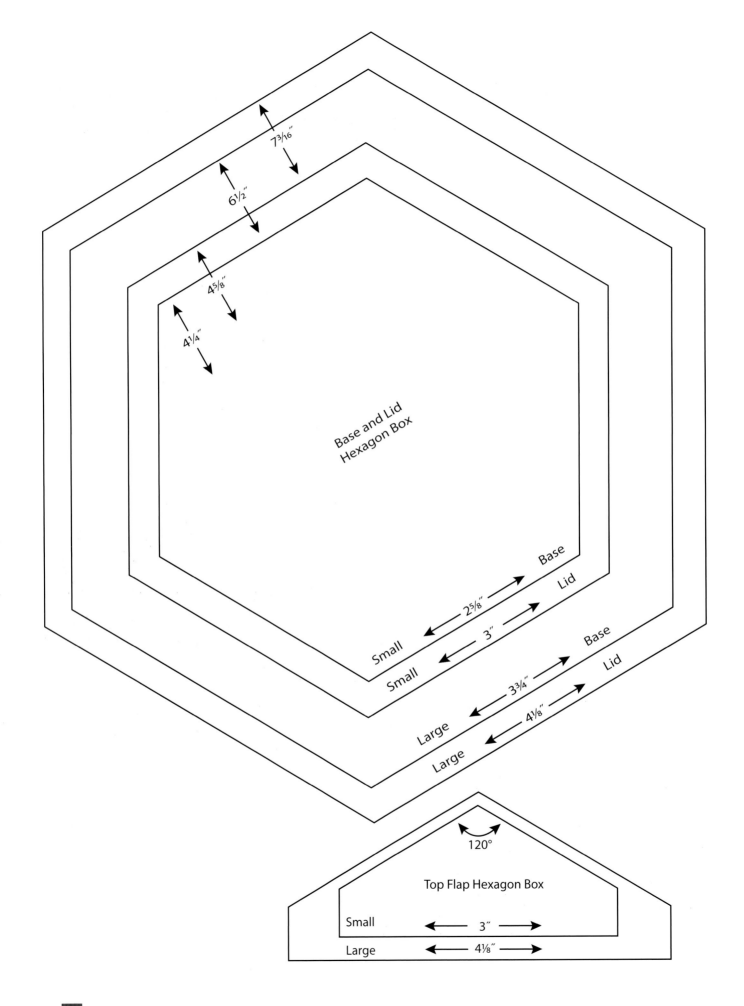

Base and Lid
Hexagon Box

7³⁄₁₆″

6½″

4⁵⁄₈″

4¼″

Base
Lid
Small — 2⁵⁄₈″
Small — 3″
Base
Lid
Large — 3¾″
Large — 4⅛″

120°

Top Flap Hexagon Box

Small — 3″
Large — 4⅛″

DIAMOND BOX

For a jewel of a box, try this diamond box. It's sure to catch everyone's eyes and make them sparkle.

CUTTING

From stiff interfacing: Cut a 60° diamond 3½" wide for the box base, using the pattern. Cut 4 rectangles 4" × 4¾" for the sides. Cut a 60° diamond 4" wide for the lid base, using the pattern. Cut 2 rectangles 5¾" × 2¾" for the lid flaps.

To trim the lid flaps, cut the rectangles in half diagonally. Mark 4⅝" on the long straight edge (not the diagonal edge) of the triangle, and nip the corners parallel to the 2¾" side of the triangle. The length of the straight side of the piece should match the side of the diamond top.

Cut 1 fabric rectangle 16" × 18" for the box and 1 fabric square 11" × 11" for the lid from both fabrics. Cut 2 of each shape from the fusible web.

CONSTRUCTION

Using the pieces you cut for the size of box you wish to make, follow the Square Box instructions for Box Construction (page 41) and Lid Construction (page 44) to make your Diamond Box.

Sew the stiff interfacing together for the Diamond Box, fuse to the fabric, and trim the edges (2 edges trimmed).

Sew the stiff interfacing together for the Diamond Box lid, fuse to the fabric, and trim the edges (3 edges trimmed).

Cut the flaps for the Diamond Box lid.

When the lid is fused and trimmed, fold it inside out, match the edges of the stiff interfacing, and sew the corners as you did for the box. Trim these seams to ⅛" and turn the lid right side out. Finish the edges with satin stitching. You can use some Fray Check, Fray Block, or ThreadFuse on the seam after you've done the satin stitching. If you do this before stitching, it dries to a plastic and you will break needles!

> **tip** Cut your box fabric too short for the corners? Just sew the corners with a shorter stitch length, trim them to about ⅛″ from the box, and reverse the box.

> **tip** Don't want to satin stitch? Fuse and trim the inside fabric. Cut the outside fabric for your box about ½″ to ¾″ wider on each side. Fold the edges over and fuse them down before sewing the corners. Sew the corners to the inside and trim them to about ⅛″. Turn the box right side out. Voilà, no satin stitching!

> **tip** Piecing fabric? Add a second layer of fusible web after you've sewn the seams. It'll keep the seam allowance down.

VARIATIONS

Diamonds are forever, so make one for your best friend and play a little to make sure she knows it's from you.

A. Try changing the height of the sides, and use the fabric motif on the inside fabric to do some bobbin embroidery before you sew up the sides. (*Diamond Box by Linda Johansen*)

B. Piece the fabric for the top, and if you're tired of satin stitching, add some prairie points to the edge of the box. (*Diamond Box by Alex Vincent*)

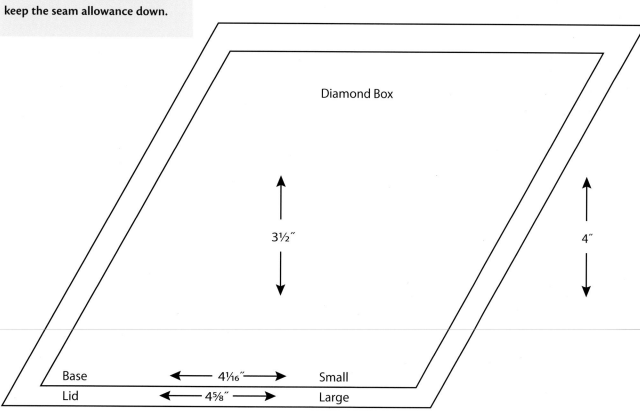

Diamond Box

3½″   4″

Base   ← 4¹⁄₁₆″ →   Small
Lid   ← 4⅝″ →   Large

TREASURE BOX

Want to give a real treasure to a special friend? Use some ornate fabrics and this box will inspire you to luscious heights! You can hide the gift inside, or make the box the gift.

CUTTING

3" × 5" Treasure Box

From stiff interfacing: Cut 3 rectangles 3" × 5" for the box base and sides. Cut 2 squares 3" × 3" for the box ends. Cut 1 rectangle 5" × 6¾" for the lid base. Trim 1 end of the lid to a point, starting 2½" in from the end. Using the pattern, cut out 2 lid ends (base length 3").

For the box, cut 1 rectangle 10" × 12" from each fabric and 2 rectangles 10" × 12" from fusible web. Cut the lid fabrics and fusible ½" larger all around the lid pieces. (Lid and box are fused separately.)

4" × 6" Treasure Box

From stiff interfacing: Cut 3 rectangles 4" × 6" for the box base and sides. Cut 2 squares 4" × 4" for the box ends. Cut 1 piece 6" × 9½" for the lid base. Trim 1 end to a point, starting 3" in from the end. Using the pattern, cut out 2 lid ends (base length 4").

For the box, cut 1 rectangle 13" × 15" from each fabric and 2 rectangles 13" × 15" from fusible web. Cut the lid fabrics and fusible ½" larger all around the lid pieces. (Lid and box are fused separately.)

CONSTRUCTION

Using the pieces you cut for the size of box you wish to make, follow the Square Box instructions for Box Construction (page 41) to make your Treasure Box. The stiff interfacing for the box portion (not the lid) is sewn together and trimmed like the Square Box, with the squares sewn onto either side of the middle rectangle. The lid is fused separately.

SHAPING

1. On the inside fabric of the box, iron firmly between the pieces of stiff interfacing where the 2 fabrics fuse to each other. This makes a visible crease line to follow when you sew the corners.

2. Fold the box diagonally, with the *inside out*. Match the corners so the adjacent sides of stiff interfacing are parallel.

3. Shorten your stitch length and sew as close as possible right along the edge of the stiff interfacing. Backstitch at the start and end.

4. With sharp scissors, trim away the excess fabric on the corners. Leave about ⅛".

5. Zigzag a length of cording around the top edge of the box, and then turn the box right side out and steam press to shape.

FINISHING

With the box right side out, satin stitch twice around the edge of the box.

MAKING THE LID

1. Fuse the 2 fabrics to the top pieces individually. Trim the fabric to the stiff interfacing shape before fusing on the second fabric. When fusing your fabric to the curved top, fuse the inside a half at a time, and use your iron to make the piece curve.

2. To iron on the second piece of fabric, curve the piece the other way over the edge of your ironing board. This reduces wrinkles in the top of the box.

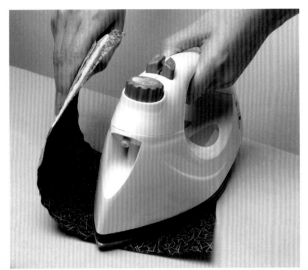

Iron a concave curve into the top as you fuse the inside fabric on. *Iron a convex curve into the top as you fuse the outside fabric on.*

3. Satin stitch the edges on each of the top pieces separately.

4. Use a mending stitch or narrow zigzag stitch to sew the rounded end pieces onto the lid top. Begin stitching on each end piece from the same side of the lid. This means that you would sew 1 side on with the lid inside out.

JOINING THE LID AND BOX

Slide both the top and the box under the machine, and sew them together along the back of the box, using a mending stitch. You may not be able to sew from corner to corner. That's okay; this is just a hinge. You can even sew it in just 2 or 3 places to make it look more like a hinge.

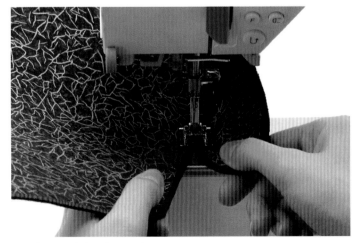

Sew the rounded ends onto the top.

A treasure box can hold anything your heart desires. Dress it up for show or down for function, or even change the basic shape. It can go anywhere!

A. I used my own hand-dyed fabric, purchased wood-grain fabric, and clipped the ends of earring posts to embellish this treasure of a steamer trunk. (*Treasure Trunk by Linda Johansen*)

B. With straps of faux suede glued on and a bevy of treasures inside, this Treasure Box would make any little girl happy for hours. (*Treasure Box by Libby Ankarberg*)

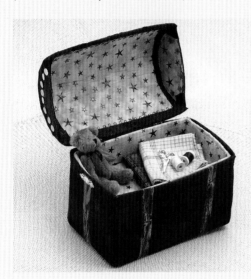

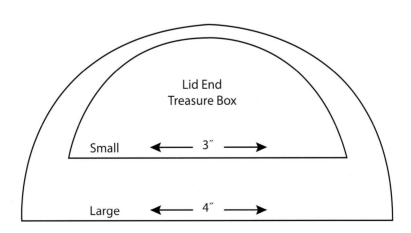

Lid End
Treasure Box

Small ← 3″ →

Large ← 4″ →

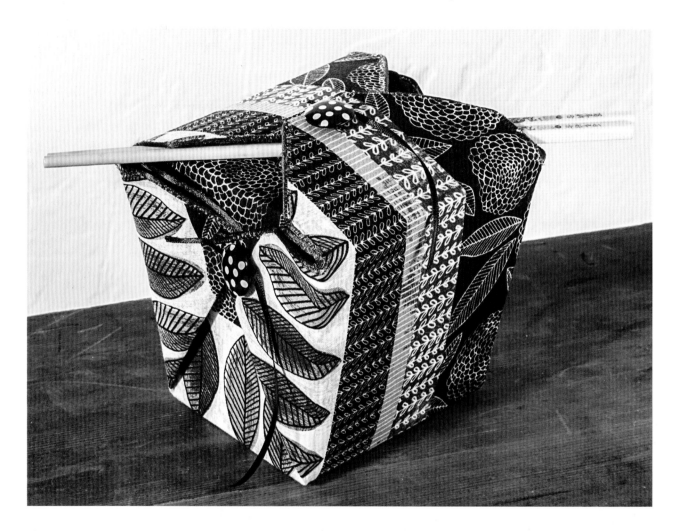

What a fun way to take your lunch to work! Unwrap the ribbons to lay the box out flat for a place mat; remember, it's washable (just be sure to prewash your fabric so it won't shrink)! Make it with heat-resistant cloth and it will even keep your food warm.

What You'll Need

- Fabric: 1 fat quarter each of 2 fabrics for small box; ⅝ yard for medium or large box
- Stiff interfacing: ¾ yard
- Fusible web: 1 yard for small box, 1½ yards for medium or large box
- 15″ square rotary ruler (12½″ square ruler works for small box)
- Thin cording or size 3 crochet thread

- 3 buttons (or 3 small hinch/hair pins, if you don't want to sew on buttons with shanks or want to remove buttons for washing) (See Resources, page 79.)
- 1 yard of ribbon or string for ties
- Overcasting or cording foot for your machine (optional)
- Patterns (pages 59 and 60)
- Basic supplies (See Materials and Supplies, page 5.)

CUTTING

Use the patterns to cut stiff interfacing for the 2 box sides, 2 box ends, 1 box base, 2 side flaps, and 2 end flaps.

Set the sewn stiff interfacing box pieces on top of 2 layers of fabric and 2 layers of fusible web. Cut a square ½″ beyond the edges.

Cut the ribbon or string in thirds.

CONSTRUCTION

Choose a size and cut the stiff interfacing and fabric. Sew the stiff interfacing pieces together as shown. Use a wide, long zigzag stitch and hold the pieces gently apart as you sew.

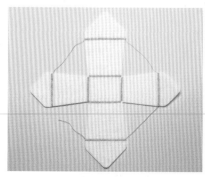

Sew the stiff interfacing together.

LAYERING

1. Iron the fusible web to the back sides of the fabric.

2. Fuse 1 layer of fabric to the stiff interfacing "cross."

3. Trim the fabric to a square, using the sides of the stiff interfacing as the outside edge.

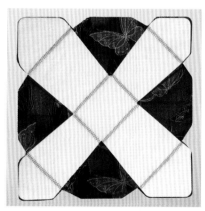

"Cross" with fabric fused and all edges trimmed. Trim each side after fusing it on. Also note the cutout (described in Step 4).

4. Make a template of the cutout piece pattern (page 59) and place it with the shortest side right beside the stiff interfacing at the side and end flaps. Cut out the small triangles on both sides of each flap. This requires reversing the template on 1 side of each lid flap.

Use the cutout piece pattern to trim the edge.

5. With a pressing sheet underneath, lay the second piece of fusible-backed fabric, fusible side down, on the reverse side of the sandwich. Make sure it is very flat, with no wrinkles underneath. Iron the fabric onto the sandwich. Be sure to fuse the 2 fabrics on the corners well (with no stiff interfacing between them). Press the iron right up to the edge of the stiff interfacing.

6. Trim the second piece of fabric the same as the first, including the cutout.

7. Zigzag cording around the edge.

SHAPING

1. Bring 2 sides of the box together and match the edges of the stiff interfacing on 1 end. Pin just off the edge of the stiff interfacing. Iron a crease in the fused fabric.

Pin the corner, and then iron a crease.

2. Fold and crease all the corners in the same way.

3. Overlap the corners at the ends, and pin them together to hold the box.

4. Mark a spot on the outside fold, ½″ in from the fold, for the button. Mark another spot on the underneath fold, about 1″ away from the first spot, for ribbon placement.

Use pins to mark the placement for the ribbons and buttons.

5. Fold in the side flaps. Fold in the lid end flaps over the side flaps, and mark each flap about ½″ from the edges that meet. This will be the placement for the button and ribbon on the top. Wrapping the ribbon or string around the button will hold the box together while you are carrying things in it.

6. Unpin the box corners, and sew on the buttons and ribbons where they are marked.

> *tip* **In traditional to-go boxes, the side flaps fold in last, but I find that folding the side flaps in first works better to keep the box square while traveling. Fold it up, fill it, and then go to lunch!**

VARIATIONS

Whether you're taking a lunch, going on a picnic, or giving a gift, these sweet boxes will carry the day.

A. Fuse or sew a binding around the edge, and add handles to this lower, wider variation, and you have a great way to do takeout. I used stretchy wrapping cord for the closures on this box. *(Lunch Box by Linda Johansen)*

B. This bandana box with matching coasters and napkin shows how it converts into a place mat. *(Bandana Box by Linda Johansen)*

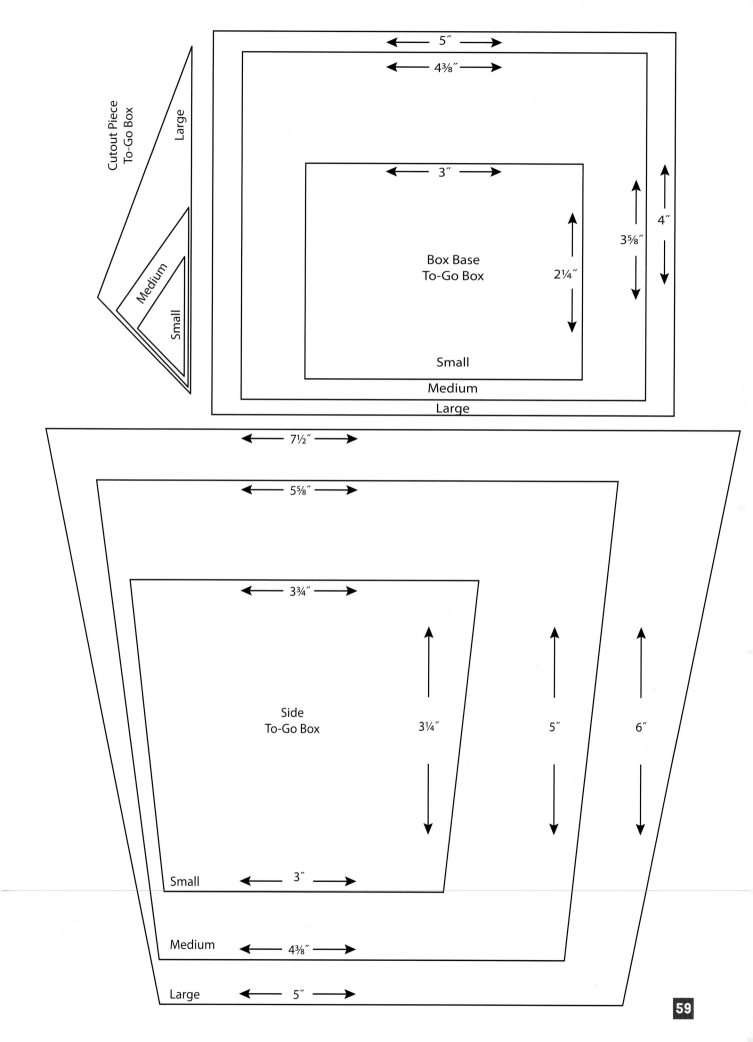

Cutout Piece
To-Go Box

Large

Medium

Small

5″

4⅜″

3″

Box Base
To-Go Box

2¼″

3⅝″

4″

Small

Medium

Large

7½″

5⅝″

3¾″

Side
To-Go Box

3¼″

5″

6″

Small 3″

Medium 4⅜″

Large 5″

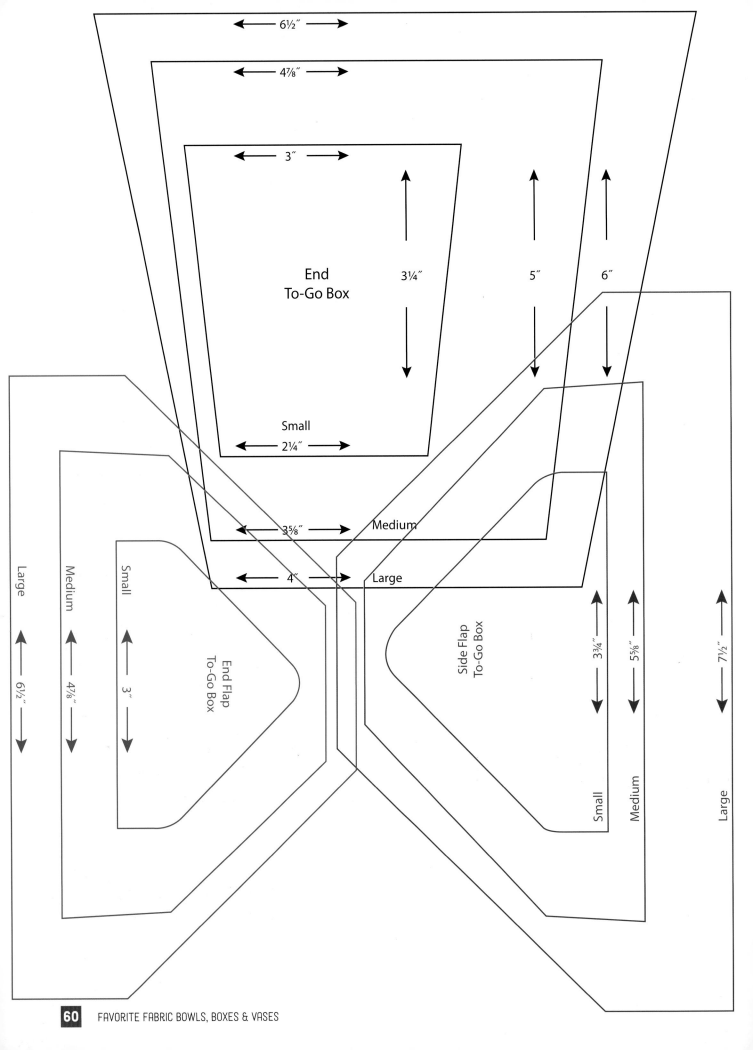

6½″

4⅞″

3″

End
To-Go Box

3¼″   5″   6″

Small

2¼″

Medium

3⅝″

Large

4″

Side Flap
To-Go Box

Large

Medium

Small

End Flap
To-Go Box

6½″   4⅞″   3″

Small   Medium   Large

3¾″   5⅝″   7½″

One of the first questions many of you will have is, "How can I use the vases?" Obviously, you can't put water in them, but you can put a small shot glass or recycled glass jar with a flower frog (used for flower arranging) inside to hold real flowers from your garden. You can also use silk flowers with some stones or marbles in the bottom, or try some feathers and grass stalks—or, better yet, make some fabric flowers of your own. You can even make the base without a bottom and put it over a glass or plastic container.

vases

This classy vase, with its simple, clean lines and a bit of embellishment, is just the thing for holding spring flowers.

LAYERING

1. Cut the stiff interfacing and a piece of each fabric to 12½″ × 12½″. If you are not using fast2fuse, you will also need to cut 2 pieces of fusible web 12½″ × 12½″.

2. Lightly fuse the first piece of fabric to the stiff interfacing.

3. Turn the sandwich over, and fuse the second piece of fabric to the other side.

4. Press firmly, and be sure all the edges are fused well on both sides.

CUTTING THE VASE

1. Trim the edges of the square sandwich to square it up. Trim as little as possible to get clean edges and square corners.

2. Cut an 8″-wide strip from the square; then cut this strip into 4 pieces 8″ × 2½″. These will be the sides of the vase.

EMBELLISHING THE SIDES

CUTTING AND PREPARING

1. From the remaining sandwich pieces, cut 1 base square 2½″ × 2½″, and cut 3 strips ¾″ wide along the longest side. Cut these strips into pieces ¾″ × 2¾″, ¾″ × 3¾″, ¾″ × 4½″, and ¾″ × 5½″.

2. From the same fabric that you used for the inside of the vase, cut 1 piece 7″ × 8″.

3. Cut a similar piece of fusible web, and iron it to the back of the fabric.

4. Cut the fusible-backed fabric into 4 strips 7″ × 2″.

5. Center 1 small embellishment piece on a strip of fused fabric. You can fuse to either side of the piece, because the back won't show.

6. Hold the piece in position as you turn it over and fuse the fabric to the piece.

7. Repeat this for each small piece.

8. Trim the edges of each piece so the fabric is ½″ wider on each side and ⅜″ longer on each end.

9. Fold the short ends over the sandwich, and fuse the excess fabric to just the sandwich. Tuck the extra fabric on the end down next to the sandwich, and press. This allows the longer edge to overlap and still be shorter than the sandwich.

Tuck the sides of the end flap in a bit to get a good corner.

10. Fold the long sides over to the back, and iron them down.

ATTACHING THE PIECES

1. Place the sides next to each other on a table. Place an embellishment piece on each side to decide where you want to position the embellishments—these pieces will look better if they are not centered either vertically or horizontally.

2. Sew the embellishment pieces in place, 1 at a time, topstitching about 1⁄16″ inside the edge. Use a needle-down position to turn the corner, and shorten the length of the straight stitch to lock your stitches at the end.

3. Cut 4 pieces of ribbon or yarn, each 9″ long.

4. Center a piece of yarn or ribbon over the small embellishment piece, and sew the end with a shortened straight stitch right at the end of the side piece. Be sure this stitching is close enough to the edge so that later satin stitching will cover it.

5. Twist the ribbon a few times (or none at all for 1 or 2 sides). Tack down the loose end of the ribbon by stitching very close to the edge of the piece with a short straight stitch.

ADDING THE BASE

1. Place the sides in the order you want them.

2. Sew them to the base with a 4.0-width, 1.5-length zigzag stitch. Keep the embellished side up so that the ribbon doesn't flatten as you sew.

Zigzag the sides to the base, with the embellishments facing up.

3. Zigzag cording onto all the edges, using the same stitch setting as in Step 2. (Refer to Using Cording, page 9, as needed.)

4. Satin stitch over the cording with a 4.0-width, 0.2-length stitch.

5. Satin stitch around the base with the same settings as above.

SHAPING

1. Fold the vase in half, with 2 adjacent sides together, to sew the sides. Sew the outside edges only.

Fold the vase in half.

2. Starting at the top, zigzag down the side with a 1.5-width, 1.5-length stitch. Backstitch at the beginning and end of the seam, and make sure the top edges are even; you can pin them if you want. The right side of the stitch should go just barely to the right of the pieces, and the left side should just catch both pieces.

3. Fold each of the last 2 sides together, and sew 1 at a time. It's okay to bend the stiff interfacing; you can steam it to shape later. Remember to backstitch at both the top and the bottom.

Scrunch the vase to get the last edges under the presser foot.

4. Steam the sides and bottom to shape, being careful not to steam the ribbon flat.

Straight sides often fell by the wayside with this vase. It was just too much fun to play with all the options.

A. Skinny, concave sides make for a more ethereal feeling. *(Tall Vase by Kim Campbell)*

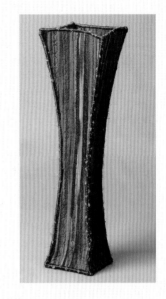

B. Make the sides slightly convex, and add different embellishments. This completely changes the style of the vase. *(Paper Vase by Linda Johansen)*

GINGER JAR VASE

This sweet little vase is so easy—you won't believe it! Slip some weights inside and try filling it with your favorite feathers instead of flowers.

What You'll Need

- Fabric: 2 fat quarters of coordinating fabrics, or 2 scraps same size as stiff interfacing (If using same fabric inside and out, use 1 fat quarter for small vase or ⅓ yard for large vase.)

- Stiff interfacing: 1 piece 5½″ × 15″ and 1 piece 2½″ × 2½″ for small vase; 1 piece 8″ × 16″ and 1 piece 2½″ × 2½″ for large vase (I recommend fast2fuse for this vase for its ease of fusing and flexibility.)

- ¾ yard of fusible web (or 1⅛ yards, if not using fast2fuse)

- Thread to match fabrics

- Template plastic (optional)

- Sturdy balloon

- Patterns (page 69)

- Basic supplies (See Materials and Supplies, page 5.)

LAYERING

1. Cut a piece of fabric 16″ × 6″ for the small vase or 17″ × 7½″ for the large vase—this fabric will be on the inside of your vase. (If not using fast2fuse, cut 1 piece of fusible web the same size as the fabric.)

2. Fuse the fabric to 1 side of the stiff interfacing. Press firmly, and test to be sure all the corners and edges are fused well. (If not using fast2fuse, apply fusible web to the back of the fabric first.)

3. Cut a piece of fabric 23″ × 7″ for the small vase or 23″ × 10½″ for the large vase—this fabric will be on the outside of your vase. Cut a piece of fusible web the same size as the fabric. Apply fusible web to the back of the fabric piece, and set aside for now.

CUTTING THE VASE

1. Trace the side piece and base patterns (page 69) onto template plastic, and cut them out. Trace 6 sides and 1 base onto the stiff interfacing sandwich.

Trace the pattern on the fabric 6 times.

2. Cut out all the pieces. I like to use a rotary cutter. However, on inside corners, I use small sharp scissors.

tip **Fussy cut the outer fabric for the sides of the ginger jar. It takes a bit more fabric, but what a great look!**

tip **Cut out 6 patterns from freezer paper, and iron them on the fabric side of the sandwich to cut around. Be gentle when pulling them off!**

tip **Use a sturdy French curve to rotary cut the sides. That's what I used to draw them!**

3. Lay the stiff interfacing pieces on the second piece of fabric, and cut around each, leaving the fabric a generous ½″ wider on all sides and ¾″ across the top.

Cut a generous ½″ all around, plus ¾″ across the top.

4. With the fabric side up, center each sandwich piece on the fabric piece under it, and carefully turn it over and fuse it on.

5. Clip straight in toward the inside corners at the neck of the vase side.

6. Fold in the sides, and fuse them to the back of each piece. Pull them snugly against the edge as you fold them over.

7. Trim a bit off each corner of the fused fabric, and tuck the edge in so that there is more fusible surface to hold the top and bottom as you fold it over and fuse. This also ensures that the folded-over edges are inside the edges of the whole piece.

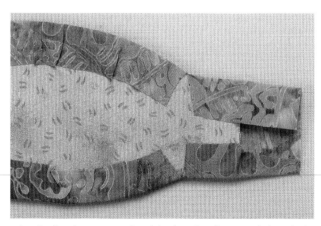

Trim the fused corners and tuck in the edges for a good clean look.

ADDING THE BASE

1. Set your machine for a zigzag stitch (1.5–2.0 width, 1.5 length). Check your stitches and tension on a scrap of stiff interfacing with fabric fused on both sides.

2. Place 1 side at a time on the base, with the bottom edge of the side even with 1 side of the base. Inside fabrics will be face to face. I like to sew 2 or 3 stitches in place at the start and end of each piece.

3. Continue around the base, zigzagging each side. You will need to open each piece out before you sew on the next one.

Zigzag the sides to the base.

SHAPING

1. Set your machine for a zigzag stitch (1.5–2.0 width, 1.5 length).

2. Fold 2 adjacent sides together, with the fabrics you want inside the vase facing each other.

3. Pin the top edge of the vase so that it stays even.

Pin the top edge to keep it even.

4. Hold the sides together while you zigzag the edge. The outside stitch of the zigzag should go over the edge of the 2 sides, and the inside stitch should just catch the edge of the fabric around the sides.

5. Be sure to do some extra stitches in each inside corner and at the top and bottom edges to strengthen them.

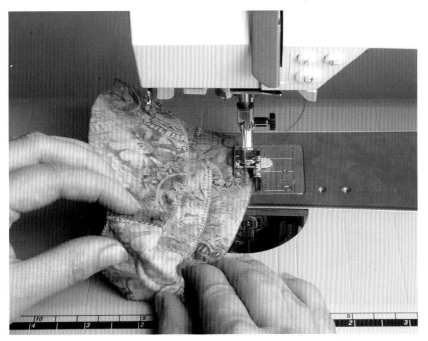

Use a narrow zigzag to stitch the sides together.

FINISHING

1. Push the sides of the vase out to the shape you like, and steam iron just a bit to help shape it. Use a balloon, or shape it with your fingers as it cools.

2. Steam iron the base, and then set it on something flat while it cools.

VARIATIONS

Once you've made one vase, forget the instructions and make another any way you like. Play with the shape, the materials, and the embellishments.

A. A five-sided base with a fussy-cut handkerchief (mistakenly sewn inside out, then turned) made for a fun shape. (*Handkerchief Vase by Linda Johansen*)

B. Fussy cutting fabrics with motifs adds a definite theme to the vase. (*Geisha Vase by Linda Johansen*)

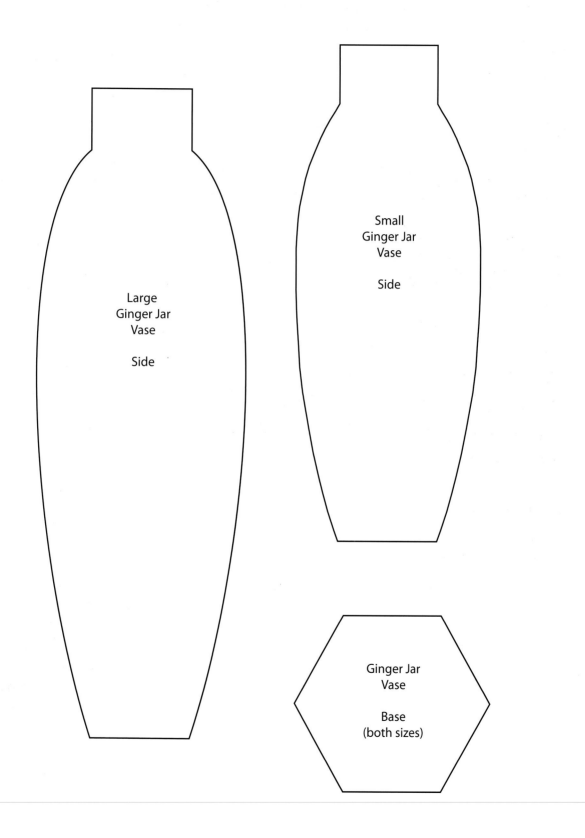

Large
Ginger Jar
Vase

Side

Small
Ginger Jar
Vase

Side

Ginger Jar
Vase

Base
(both sizes)

CLASSIC VASE

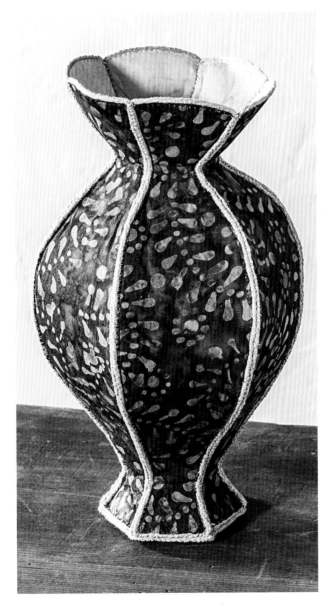

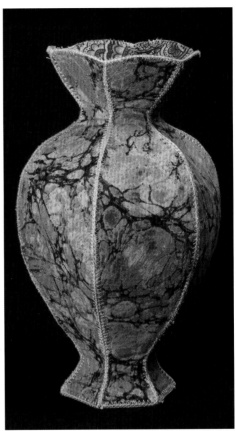

Elegant, classy lines. Stylish, graceful fabric. Small or tall. Any way you cut it, this vase is easy to make. Put it on the mantel or on the center of the table—it will be a winner.

MAKING THE PATTERN

1. Trace the side and base patterns onto template plastic.

2. Cut out the side template, being careful to keep both edges symmetrical.

3. Cut out the base template.

LAYERING

1. Cut 1 piece 16½″ × 10″ and 1 piece 3″ × 3″ from each fabric.

2. Fuse a piece of fabric to 1 side of the stiff interfacing. (If not using fast2fuse, apply fusible web to the back of the fabric pieces first.)

3. Iron the second piece of fabric onto the other side of the stiff interfacing. Use a rotary cutter and ruler to trim the long edge of the stiff interfacing sandwich.

4. Repeat this for the 3″ base piece.

MARKING AND CUTTING

1. Place the vase template on 1 side of the large sandwich piece, and draw around it 6 times for the sides and once on the 3″ square for the base. Draw on the inside fabric or cut just inside the drawn lines so that the lines don't show on the finished vase.

2. Using sharp scissors or a small rotary cutter, cut out the pieces.

 Change the shape—bigger curves equal a more voluptuous shape.

 Fuse an extra decorative piece of fabric onto the side(s) before constructing the vase.

STITCHING THE SIDES

1. Zigzag colored or decorative cording on each side. Start at the top of 1 side, and sew cording down that side, across the bottom, and then up the next side. Use a 4.0-width, 1.5-length stitch, and backstitch at the start and end. Don't put cording on the top edge or satin stitch yet! (Refer to Using Cording, page 9, as needed.)

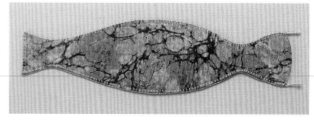

Zigzag decorative cording onto the sides.

2. Zigzag some of the same cording around the base piece.

3. If you want to (or if your cording doesn't match your fabric well), you can satin stitch all the sides after you add the cording.

tip **If you make this one out of canvas, be sure to do a lot of quilting to hold the sides together.**

ADDING THE BASE

1. Place the bottom of a side piece next to 1 side of the base piece. Place the outside fabric up on all of the pieces.

2. Zigzag these pieces together using a 1.5-width, 1.5-length stitch. Stitch in place at the beginning and end of each piece as you add it.

3. Continue placing the bottoms of the side pieces next to the base, and zigzag around the base until all 6 are attached.

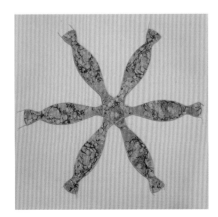

Satin stitch the side pieces to the base.

SHAPING

1. Fold 2 adjacent sides together with the fabrics that you want inside the vase facing each other.

2. Pin the top edges to make sure they will match.

Fold the vase in half, pin the top edge, and zigzag the edge.

3. Sew from the top of the vase down the side to the bottom, using a narrow, short-length zigzag (1.5–2.0 width, 1.5 length). Backstitch at the start and finish to hold the seams well.

4. Sew 2 seams while the piece is flat, and then continue matching sides and zigzagging them together. You will need to scrunch the stiff interfacing to match the sides.

Carefully zigzag up the sides.

FINISHING

1. Trim the edges even, if necessary, and zigzag cording around the lip. Stop frequently to "roll" the vase, and don't be afraid to scrunch the vase to get most of it out of the way while you sew around the lip.

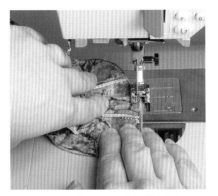

Zigzag the cording around the lip of the vase.

tip **If a side seam pulls apart a bit on the lip, pull gently and firmly on the cording as you zigzag to pull the edges together. You should restitch big pull-aparts before applying the cording!**

2. If you want (or if the cording does not match well), satin stitch around the lip after you add the cording.

tip **Patch fabrics together for a real quilted vase. Iron fusible web onto the fabrics before sewing them together and after. Carefully iron down the seam allowances so that they don't puff up when ironed to the fast2fuse. (Use 2 layers of fusible web if using Timtex.) Fussy cut the sides if you want them to match exactly.**

STEAMING

1. Blow up a large, sturdy balloon inside the vase.

2. Steam the vase to shape while the balloon is full, and leave in the balloon while the fabric cools. (Refer to Basic Techniques, Shaping, page 12, as needed).

3. Steam the base, and gently press it on something flat to cool.

(Refer to Basic Techniques, Shaping, page 12, as needed).

VARIATIONS

Play with the curves a bit—just a small change in the shape can make a big difference in the finished appearance.

A. Widening the pattern and deepening the curves creates a voluptuous vase! (*Voluptuous Canvas Vase by Sidnee Snell*)

B. Lengthening the neck using very modern fabric with canvas interfacing, and then pushing the neck down inside, makes a vase with an unusual shape. (*Modern Vase by Kim Campbell*)

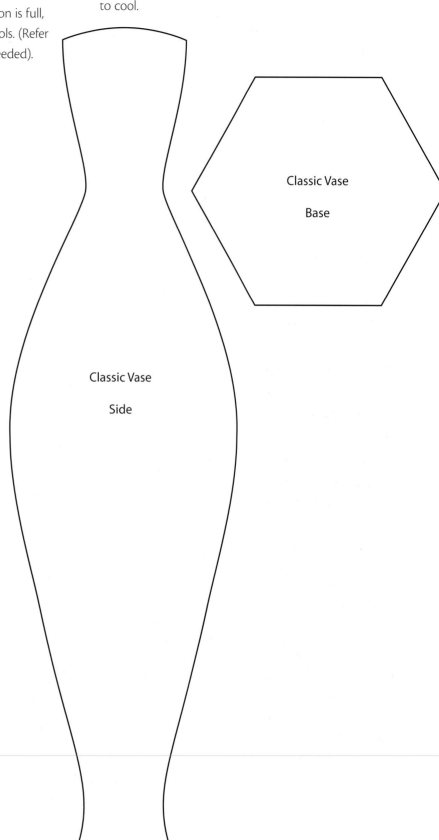

Classic Vase
Base

Classic Vase
Side

There's nothing fishy about this vase (unless, of course, you choose fishy fabric). It looks great done in any fabric for a simple, elegant vase.

CUTTING AND FUSING

1. Cut 2 pieces of stiff interfacing 6¼″ × 7½″ and 1 piece 2″ × 3½″ for the small bowl, or 2 pieces 8″ × 9½″ and 1 piece 3″ × 4½″ for the large bowl.

2. Cut 2 pieces each of inside and outside fabric 6¼″ × 7½″ and 1 of each 2″ × 3½″ for the small bowl, or cut 2 of each 8″ × 9½″ and 1 of each 3″ × 4½″ for the large bowl. (Be aware of any directional designs on your fabric. If you are using fish, they swim better right side up!)

3. Fuse the inside fabric pieces to 1 side of each stiff interfacing piece. (If not using fast2fuse, apply fusible web to the back of the fabric first.)

4. Fuse the outside fabric pieces to the other side of the stiff interfacing pieces.

5. Trace the side and base patterns onto template plastic, and cut out.

6. On the inside fabric, trace 2 sides and 1 base on the fabric sandwich pieces, and cut them out. Be aware of any directional designs on your fabric.

STITCHING THE SIDES

1. Zigzag the cording around each piece, using a 4.0-width, 1.5-length stitch. (Refer to Using Cording, page 9, as needed.)

2. Satin stitch around each piece individually.

SHAPING

1. Set your machine for a narrow zigzag stitch (1.5 width, 1.5 length) to sew the sides to the base.

2. Align the corner edge of the elliptical base with the bottom edge of a vase side. Keep the base on top while sewing, and make sure the edges match as you go. The right stitch of the zigzag should go out over the edge of the pieces. You want to just catch the edge of the satin stitching on both pieces.

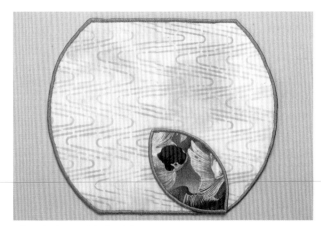

Align the base with the side.

3. Start by sewing several stitches in place, or backstitching. Pull the base to meet the edge of the side as you sew. Backstitch at the end. The side will curl up and begin to shape as it passes under the presser foot. If the ends don't quite match, it's okay; when you sew the sides together, you can cover it.

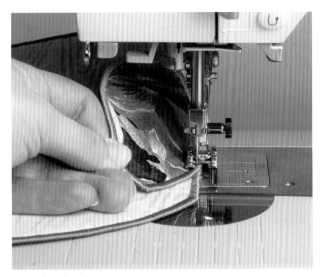

The side will curl up as you sew.

4. Sew the other side on in the same way. You will need to bend or fold the stiff interfacing to fit the vase under the presser foot. Begin sewing at the opposite end of the base that you started from with the first side.

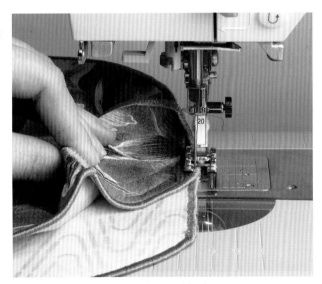

Scrunch the vase as you sew the second side.

tip **Before sewing the vase, use scraps to cut an ellipse shape, and practice adding sides to it if you want to see what will happen.**

5. Fold the 2 halves together, and pin the top edge on 1 side.

6. Begin sewing down the side from the top. You will need to fold the base in half to do this. Remember to backstitch at the beginning and end of the seam.

FINISHING

1. Steam iron the base first, and hold it on something flat until it's cool and holds the shape you want.

2. Steam iron the sides as necessary. I usually like to steam the top opening a bit rounder than it wants to be without shaping. Just hold it in the shape you want it, or place something round in it while it cools.

Save your fingers and use a glass, a jar, or a ball of string to help steam the lip to a round shape.

Everyone will comment on this fishbowl, even if you don't put fish in it! You don't even have to keep it elliptical.

A. Two rectangles and a freehand-cut, sort-of-elliptical base were embellished with stitching before assembly for this sensuously shaped canvas art vase. *(Freehand-Cut Vase by Kim Campbell)*

B. By adding width to the base and two extra sides, you can have an even more realistic fish bowl. *(Dolphin Vase by Linda Johansen)*

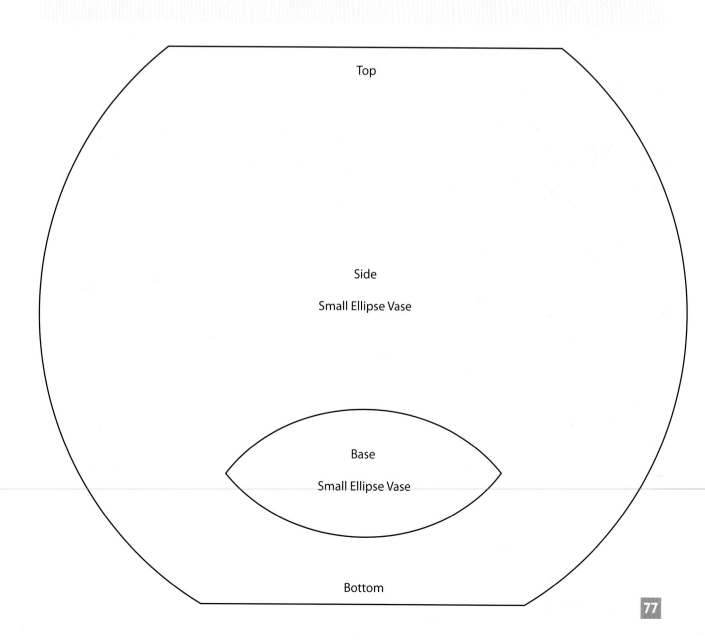

Top

Side

Small Ellipse Vase

Base

Small Ellipse Vase

Bottom

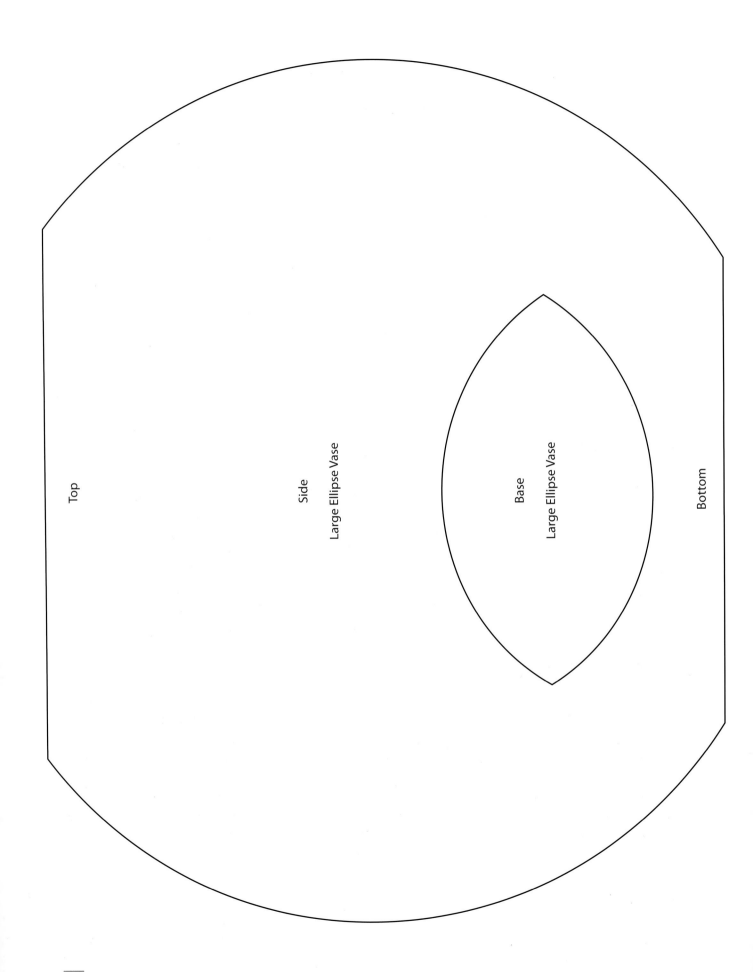

Top

Side

Large Ellipse Vase

Base

Large Ellipse Vase

Bottom

RESOURCES

Clearview Triangle rulers; fast2fuse Double-Sided Fusible Stiff Interfacing (Light, Medium, or Heavy)**; Timtex**

- C&T Publishing
  ctpub.com

- Also available at your local quilt store

Wonder-Under

- Pellon
  pellonprojects.com > search Wonder-Under

- Available at most quilt and sewing stores

Omnigrid rotary cutters and rulers

- Prym-Dritz
  dritz.com

Isacord Thread

Large spools carry 1,000 meters. Small spools, which carry 200 meters, are sold as Mettler Polysheen.

- Oklahoma Embroidery Supply & Design (OESD)
  embroideryonline.com

- Or ask your local quilt store to carry it

Fabrics

Most of the samples in this book were made with fabrics from the following companies. Ask for them at your local quilt store!

- Classic Cottons
  exclusivelyquilters.com

- Robert Kaufman Fabrics
  robertkaufman.com

- RJR Fabrics
  rjrfabrics.com

- Timeless Treasures
  ttfabrics.com

ABOUT THE AUTHOR

Linda Johansen is the author of these other C&T books:

- *The Fabric Dyer's Dictionary*
- *Fast, Fun & Easy Christmas Decorations*
- *Fast, Fun & Easy Fabric Bowls*
- *Fast, Fun & Easy Fabric Boxes*
- *Fast, Fun & Easy Fabric Vases*
- *Fast, Fun & Easy Irresist-A-Bowls*

She lives in Corvallis, Oregon, with her husband and three border collies.

For her first five books, she has had the help of a very special and creative group of women who deserve a lot of credit for everything from the details of editing and making how-to samples to the fun of working out the design ideas and construction. You've seen their names and creations; now Linda would like you to meet them.

GUEST ARTISTS

Libby Ankarberg began quilting nineteen years ago when she left civil engineering to raise a family, which now includes three teenagers and two dogs. Never one to do things by the book, she finds that both her fabric art and glass fusing provide an outlet for her love of color and texture.

Kim Campbell feels that the older she gets, the more certain she is that everyone needs a playgroup. She values the opportunity to get together and play and create—to work with others in a collaborative effort, exploring the challenges, enjoyment, and satisfaction of making art. And she'll do anything to get out of satin stitching!

Sidnee Snell goes straight for her sewing machine (not a blankie or teddy bear or even chocolate) when looking for comfort. She has been sewing since she was a kid, and the sound of a sewing machine is familiar. When not quilting, she enjoys tap dancing and singing off-key in the shower. See more of her work at sidneesnell.com.

Alex Vincent, a former molecular biologist (studying octopus genes), began her quilting with a group of women making raffle quilts for her children's school. Enjoyment of the company of her family and friends, and delight in the beauty of the natural world, influences her textile work.